Unfold
Your Petals

Unfold Your Petals

VANGE CAIN

Ordering Information:

For orders and inquiries, please contact:
1-888-404-1388
www.goldtouchpress.com
book.orders@goldtouchpress.com

Printed in the United States of America

Appreciation

As I unfold my petals I open my heart to say thank you so much for participating in this moment with me. Your continued support has kept me going. I heard your warm whispers and my petals spread far and wide to the people by my side.

Cliff Pierre - In the moments of fear, you took my hand and said," Follow me." We ended up at that place we are today. We began to build something solid from the emptiness of nothing. We had no idea where we would end up, but we did it anyway. Many times I have doubted my own capability and it was you who believed in me. It was you who made me recognize the girl in the mirror when I barely knew myself. You held the mirror to my reflection so I could see all I can become. It was my first public video that you played back for me to see. I ran out the house and you said," Hey come back; It was you who held my hand and said," I want you to see all the potential you have."

Gaylene Simmons - To a long lost friend who sends her love over the sea for me. Thank you for telling all your friends about my book. It was very helpful. Thanks so much for supporting me.

Kelly Barteaux - To the fabulous lady who once was my grade seven teacher and who has travelled with me through many life times. The woman who inspires so many students to be their best. How does it feel my dear, to know your former student published a book and that you are part of it. Sounds like destiny to me. Thank you for editing this book my sweet friend.

Destiny Cain - To the loving daughter who always supports me. Thanks so much you are lovely.

Julie Cain: Aunt Julie. I apologize that I forgot to add you to my last book please forgive me. Today, I send you all my love. Thank you for supporting me.

Shataz Cain Beals - To the son who just rocks my world. Thanks so much for always listening.

Baskaran Ratnam - To the man who supports me on my journey. Thanks for assisting me with photography. It is always a pleasure to work with a perfect gentlemen.

Andrew Mussington - To the cool guy who didn't just assist me with photography, but who is an awesome friend. Thanks for lending your wards of wisdom when I need them.

Suzy Tamasay - To the leading lady who took me under her wing and showed me what the modelling world was all about. Thanks for believing in me. Your appearance in my life shaped the woman I've become today.

Tony Fera - To the man who has supported me on this journey. My dream wouldn't have come true without you. It was you who published my first book and gave me the kick start I needed for success. Thanks so much for all you've done for me and the community. You are a very highly respected man.

Christian Jones - Thank you so much for your continued devotion in regards to publishing this book.

Olimpia Elena Tulpan - For your continued support with the submission of photos. Not only am I thanking you for your support, but also for being a dear friend.

I would like to give thanks to 'The Book Walker' for discovering my book amidst the many books that are floating around on the internet. I humbly thank you for writing such amazing words. It is such a liberating feeling when I put myself out there and I am acknowledged. I guess now is my turn to pay it forward and it starts with thank you.

❀ Book Talk

In her book Unfold Your Petals, Evangeline Cain beckons to the goddess in every woman. Cain examines the ways of the goddess and her timeless impact in a woman's everyday life, which, ultimately, ripples to affect the whole universe.

The author empowers every woman to look at herself and see the goddess waiting to be set free. A woman herself is a universe going through millions of transitions and transformations. She goes through ups and downs and twists and turns. Marred by the conflicts surrounding her, she often hinders herself from becoming who she is always meant to be, allowing herself to settle far from her goddess nature. This is where Cain wants women to pause and carefully examine themselves against their real goddess nature. According to the author, voices that cry out, "I'm not skinny enough. He will never love me. I have stretch marks," are the voices that stop women from experiencing love on a deeper level. "Not your looks or your stretch marks. It's you standing in your own way because you've already told yourself: 'I am not worthy of his love.'"

Cain cites her own experiences to illustrate her points. She is honest and open about her weaknesses and victorious when she said, "Feminism in a goddess leads to a man's soul. It leads deep into the walls that many are afraid to go." To help women understand their own nature, the author provides a shortlist of myth goddesses from all over the world. She gives historical information about these goddesses and helps readers understand how these goddesses may be called upon to protect, heal, or help women in the modern times.

The rest of the book is devoted to the development of the inner goddess found in every woman. Distributed over thirty days are topics for the mind, body, and spirit, every single one of which will surely help a woman discover herself and her potentials.

Unfold Your Petals by Evangeline Cain oozes with feminism, empowerment, and hope. It is a powerful reminder of a woman's power to be the goddess that she is meant to be.

-The BookWaler

Sharing another empowering message to women all over the world, author Evangeline Cain talks about the embodied woman in her book, Unfold Your Petals.

This book is about the challenges that women go through in life and encourages women to call on ancient goddesses to aid them in their time of need. Cain reminds women that they are not alone, no matter what the world would rather them believe. It upholds the truth that the goddesses of ancient times who have seen the world from when it is very young until its recent evolution want women to succeed. It is up to the women of today to call upon them and embody what these goddesses represent.

Unfold your Petals help women understand who these goddesses are and how they move through the world. It aims to help women understand all aspects of being a goddess, including their gentleness and strength.

There are many nuances to womanhood and femininity that most people do not explore. Perhaps, it is because the world has conditioned us to think that being a woman means being the weaker gender. Or, because femininity is beautiful, that is all it is good for. So many women and men do not understand the strength that comes with being a woman and a goddess. It is for this reason that so many women hide who they are, what they think, and how they feel. They fear that these essential parts of who they are make them seem vulnerable. We live in a culture that tells us that vulnerability equals weakness. This can't be further from the truth.

Throughout the book, Cain encourages women to open up. She believes that "each of our petals represents our accomplishments that have nurtured our wounds and what we can't nurture the goddesses carry us through." In this book are thirty days of devotion and knowledge to help women understand and harness the power of their thoughts, feelings, and identity.

Reviews and What Readers Say

"Profound and pleasurable read that offers explanation of our natural tendency and social behavior. Unfold Your Petals is a notable work worth a space on your shelf."

Allow the goddess to love you endlessly.

She the goddess has called you in... into her sacred heart. She holds space for you my loves and even when you feel like you are alone in an empty space, she is there with open arms. As I call out to the goddesses, I ask that their truth live out through me and carry on to you. The goddesses' hearts are calling us to awaken; to slowly step forth and claim the love in you that went hiding- that part of you that fell apart or maybe forgot her truth. The goddesses and our ancestors left behind an oath that asks us to carry love in our lineage and to hold this love in our DNA for all of humanity to feel. If we listen, she lives in our hearts. She is with us every step of the way. Every breath UKwe take; and every fibre that sheds from our soul is dusted upon her memory that can't be erased. In this voice of the goddess we honour the masculine too. My loves, we do not exclude you, for many of you held the medicine that led the way. You held the sacred Rose in your heart for her; you stood beside her so she could flourish. You went nowhere as she found her way. You carried her to the altar of self- love when you felt herself fade away.

Chapter 1

Celestial blessings and welcome my loves to the activation of mother Gia's love that is presented by Evangeline also known as Vange. I am a writer and my gift has always been to bring the goddess to you.

❁ Venus

I am the representation of goddesses & their love. Therefore, all that I bring to you is the truth and a treasure you can hold onto. I pour onto you mamas love and the protected embodiment that lives inside her body. She asks," that you re-energize the sacred feminine that resides in you in order to heal the sacred masculine. As you accept this gift you find balance between the feminine and masculine energies. In accepting this process you are choosing to be a part of this evolution through letting the fears that reside in you to fade away. To let go of the old beliefs that aren't serving the goddess in you. A woman who chooses to hide away from the mirror of herself hinders her ascension process and is disconnected from the sacred feminine principal.

Mother Venus is asking you to rise from the deep slumber of who you thought you were, so you visit with the sacred feminine once and for all. To discover the light that is roaring inside of her that has the power to pull you away from prisons that have held you captive to destruction that wasn't yours to claim. I am the rose who's risen from the coils of the earth and I live inside each and everyone of you. I show my thorns only to those who deny my existence for the blood that will be drowned joins you in sisterhood. I have been born as a goddess, born from the foam of the earth. The deepest darkest parts of the abyss and I have been born again and brought to earth to call it my place of love.

As ambassador of the goddess, I need you to understand that the earth is calling us to bring peace to the earth. Listen to me my daughters from the foreign land of Libyan. A mirage - place of palm trees and olive gardens that merge out of the sand. She will rise again just as beautiful as the place that she came from. She shall not stay buried in the sand of illusions that bury her head. Oh daughter of mine, who has traveled from Siwa and sits on the coast looking into the clear blue skies of the goddesses love. My daughters, the time is now to reveal the rose. The red curtains begin to part and she is given the chance to see freely. The above and the below must escape the illusions that the goddess is not love, for I am the light. I am dark. I am the fire that burns on and on. I am not a fountain that poisons you. I am the fountain that nourishes every fiber of your being. Every daughter that bestows upon me she arrives to find rest and love and so I shall clothe you with the spirit of the rose that has waited for your arrival. I shall nourish her and let her drink from the purity of my love. As you cross over from the abyss of my love you are guided into a place of the truth. As you pass the first imitation you shall receive your crown and be granted entry through the gates of divine love. I am the debris that's been broken down and destroyed. The remains, dragged through the storm and I swam my way to earth and I, my darlings survived. Therefore, I cry when I am misunderstood. It is only to my hero that I surrender and melt to the unfolding within the bud of my yoni, because he is my husband. He is my love. He rides the waves of my heart, calling to me from the west winds and as he screams out my name he shall find me waiting for him ready to unfold the rose buds that have been lost to him. He has been on a journey, trying to undertake the destroyer and he rises to stand tall against the demands of destruction. There I am the barrier of love with open arms waiting for him. There is an urgency for his power, to water the goddesses soil as she has cried tirelessly. I have nurtured the earth with my tears. Inside of him is an eye of direction that shines so bright. A light I shall follow like the moonlight in the sky. He shall not deny the goddess for she is the direction that leads the way to where he must go. As he explores the eyes of the lover. She is the one who loves him and nurtures him. The one who mirrors back to him that he is a hero. The lady who represents balance and justice. His living, breathing arms become my home. In the garden of my heart, I tend the flowers of our love, sown in your name. Regardless what he's done wrong my love shall never look the other way. Forever together, and forever apart, oh how he turns me on. The embers of my love always burn for you. Ordained and forged long ago by the deity of love. I see our portrait smeared over the stars. Across thousands of miles of mountains, rivers, and endless plains my love always remains the same. Together the world hums our rhythm as together we are as powerful as the sun. It is through her heart that he remembers who he is. It is through her touch that a hero shows himself. It is through her kiss that he remembers the passion that didn't exist and it is through her cry that he shall find his home. She has always been with him, feeling the pain with him. Standing at war with the lover and holding on tight. She has shed many tears for the warrior to stand tall and not run, because a man was created with the intentions of him procreating and sprouting seeds of his intentions through her. Our love is the epitome of perfection. Twin souls incarnate here on Earth to fulfill a great mission.

So he is asked to spread his powers through the earth and bring her the world for she is his existence. He must hold her high in the sky like the goddesses she is and represent the king he was created to be. She is not to be denied, but cherished for the gifts she brings. There are nightmares and destruction along their path, but it's only felt within those swimming against the tides of what is in front of them. My daughters, you have become heartbroken from the ways of the world and the way certain events played out. Don't worry my baby, for I am the wisdom. The gatekeeper who carries all the hidden mysteries untold. As I travelled the abyss I crushed the destroyer with my bare hands for harming you. As the temple meets the sky your hero comes to light as your creator. Our father cleanses your heart from all your worry. Therefore, you shall not cry anymore, but rejoice in the beauty that is yet to come. You are no longer malnourished of the feminine's essence.

You are given a new name. We shall call you goddess, but you only receive this name if you

Allow the ego to fade and stand in your power with grace. When you are naked and you face your shame a feather coat will be placed upon you. Drown yourself in the feathers of the goddesses' love that keeps you warm for you are never alone sweet one. You have been born as a goddess, born from the foam of the earth. The deepest darkest parts of the abyss and I have been born again and brought to earth to call it my place of love. I am the debris that's been broken down and destroyed. The remains, dragged through the storm and I swam my way to earth and I,my darlings survived. Therefore, I cry when I am misunderstood. It is only to my hero that I surrender and melt to the unfolding within the bud of my yoni, because he is my husband.

When the cage builds up around me that was made up of anger and rage, he was my shelter.

The walls she never allowed to tumble down was her protection. Her shield, but after some time, slowly pulling down her walls, brick by brick. She no longer felt guarded. As she unfolded, she embraced the darkest parts of her being. The shadows that terrified her no longer scared her. There's no more darkness as she reaches for the light. Pain no longer hurts her. Instead it becomes a beautiful space in which she began to love herself. This is the space of shadow integration. And this, dear ones, is how you become one with yourself.

He is my love. He rides the waves of my heart, calling to me from the west winds and as he screams out my name he shall find me waiting for him ready to unfold the rose buds that have been lost to him. He has been on a journey, trying to overcome the destroyer and he rises to stand tall against the demands of destruction. There I am the barrier of love with open arms waiting for him. There is an urgency for his power, to water the goddesses soil as she has cried tirelessly. I have nurtured the earth with my tears. Inside of him is an eye of direction that shines so bright. A light I shall follow like the moonlight in the sky.

He shall not deny the goddess for she is the direction that leads the way to where he must go. As he explores the eyes of the lover. She is the one who loves him and nurtures him. The one who mirrors back to him that he is a hero. The lady who represents balance and justice.

Together the world hums our rhythm as together we are as powerful as the sun. It is through her heart that he remembers who he is. It is through her touch that a hero shows himself. It is through her kiss that he remembers the passion that didn't exist and it is through her cry that you find your home. She has always been with him, feeling the pain with him. Standing at war with the lover and holding on tight. She has shed many tears for the warrior to stand tall and not run, because a man was created with the intentions of him procreating and sprouting seeds of his intentions through her.

He is asked to spread his powers through the earth and bring her the world for she is his existence. He must hold her high in the sky like the goddesses and represent the king he was created to be. She is not to be denied, but cherished for the gifts she brings. There are nightmares and destruction along their path, but it's only felt within those swimming against the tides of what is in front of them. My daughters, you have become heartbroken from the ways of the world and the way certain events played out. Don't worry my baby, for I am the wisdom. The gatekeeper who carries all the hidden mysteries untold. As I travelled the abyss I crushed the destroyer with my bare hands for harming you. As the temple meets the sky your hero comes to light as your creator. Our father cleanses your heart from all your worry. Therefore, you shall not cry anymore, but rejoice in the beauty that is yet to come. You are no longer malnourished of the feminine's essence. You are given a new name. We shall call you goddess, but you only receive this name if you burn your ego and stand in your power with grace. When you are naked and you face your shame a feather coat will be placed upon you. Drown yourself in the feathers of the goddesses' love that keeps you warm for you are never alone sweet one So he is asked to spread his powers through the earth and bring

Chapter 2

🌸 **Understanding the Goddess**

I am so excited to dive in and swim my way to the shore and pick up each goddess in our story line so we find our healing today. Today I will be describing the goddesses I have used for this particular book. This is so I can bring forth an understanding of who they are and the roles they impacted in society's mind. First, I want to start by describing what a goddess represents so we have some roots of her existence. A goddess is a female god, designed to rule in her feminine power—a woman recognized for her special contributions to the world. To many women, a goddess's image is very unfamiliar or hidden from their collective psyche. As a life coach, I love to see women rise out of their seat from the insight and virtue of the true goddess's being. A goddess designs her own imagination inside her mind. Her character brings forth requirements of solicitude, imagination, and courage. So let's begin to understand the goddesses I've chosen to accommodate us in our goddess therapy today. Keep in mind this book is a series, so I will not be choosing all the goddesses as characters.

❀ Aphrodite

The Greek goddess of love and fertility. She was the goddess known for her seductive ways, as all men seemed to find her loving ways extremely attractive. And we call on goddess Aphrodite to encourage us to feel love and give love.

❀ Arianrhod

The Celtic goddess of fertility. She was the goddess who stood forth to contribute to the cycles of life. Arianrhod was a Welsh Goddess who lived on an island off the west coast of Wales. At the centre of her castle was a turning glass tower, which contained the mystical Seat of Poetic Inspiration.Arianrhod, as we have noted, is a very powerful Goddess, guardian of the Seat of Poetic Inspiration and linked with the sea, the moon and the stars. She is our muse when we need creative inspiration. She is our guide to follow our dreams when our hearts are questioning our direction. What emerges from this goddess? What are we left to feel? Well, it seems, the goddess gives all women the strength to honour their bodies... The Goddess who whispers, it is safe to be a virgin and you need not cave from pressure. I believe that this wonderful Goddess Arianrhod, the beautiful woman whose feet rest on the crescent moon, and whose head is ringed with stars, is a hugely important figure in Welsh myth, and a deeply inspirational model for all women.

❀ Athena

The Greek goddess Athena entrusted in herself as a virgin goddess. She was intellectually inclined in understanding arts and literature. She was the daughter of Zeus and was created in a more unusual manner than any other goddesses, as she had no mother and sprung forth full- grown from Zeus's forehead. She was one of the bravest goddesses. She went forth in battles that concerned her town, and she jumped in headfirst toward the enemies before they could attack without a sound.

❀ Diana

The Italian goddess of fertility as she always stretched her arms to show comfort to animals and women during childbirth. She was the goddess who stepped forth to conquer conception during delivery. Diana was the goddess of great wishes, so many women went to her for blessings surrounding childbirth.

❀ Gaia

The Greek goddess of the earth, who held her children gently in her hand as she nourished the earth. She was the goddess who merged with the earth, making it a more peaceful and beautiful kingdom. Gaia is the ancestral mother who ruled the sky. She is life, the very soul of the earth. The "Mother Earth" who sprang from the heavens to love those who needed nourishment. The Roman goddess of the moon and its beautiful reflection. She controlled the underworld and magic and witchcraft and was greatly She was respected for her advice and insightful stories that directed people to a better orientation of themselves.

❋ Yemaya

Mother of the fishes. She traveled with them to distant lands to assure their safety. She was a river goddess who cared for the ocean providing support for the upper level of the sea.

❋ Diana

The Italian goddess of fertility, the moon, and the hunt. She is the goddess we call to rise when we are in the woods with wild animals that are dangerous, to show up, and to calm their thoughts, preventing harm. Diana had the power to touch animals, and they listened to her subtle voice.

❋ Rhea

The Titan goddess of fertility and motherhood. Her name means "flow" and "ease." She was the great mother who soothed women so they could flow like a river. She comforted all the lands and bestowed upon them her blessings. Goddess Rhea demonstrated she was the goddess of protection when she hid her son in a cave so he could never be found. At present, I have listed all the categories of goddesses so you will have your understanding and so you can comprehend which goddesses to call on in your particular situation. These are the magical and mystical forces of light that encourage us on our journey as we collide with their powerful vibrations, which we need right now.

❋ Lilith

In the name of heaven and in the name of earth Lilith's origins was full of mystery. She was the goddess' who represented female power and standing up for yourself. She was the guide that showed us how to reclaim the parts of ourselves that were lost. Lilith is a dangerously beautiful Goddess who refused to subordinate Herself to Adam. Lilith is the goddess who joins us with the parts of ourselves that are lost. She whispers to meet us in the dark shadows of the underworld

- in our shadow self. When an aspect of yourself is lost and we deny our primal needs we meet Lilith in the darkness of our souls, we uncover the wounds that have not healed.

Lilith gives us the strength and courage to face the wounds and bring them into the light of our conscious knowing. She helps us face all the pain, and shame held in our stories so we can embrace a new one.

Chapter 3

Who Can We Turn To

- Agricultural goddesses
- Animal goddesses
- Art goddesses
- Childhood goddesses
- Commerce goddesses
- Creator goddesses
- Destroyer goddesses
- Knowledge goddesses
- Justice goddesses
- Hunting goddesses
- Health goddesses
- Vengeance goddesses
- Underwood goddesses
- Time and fate goddesses
- Stellar fate goddesses
- Solar goddesses
- Smithing goddesses
- Peace goddesses
- Fortune goddesses
- Fire goddesses
- Fertility goddesses
- Earth goddesses
- Peace goddesses
- Oracular goddesses
- Nature goddesses
- Messenger goddesses

- Lunar goddesses
- Love and lust goddesses
- Life and death goddesses
- Night goddesses
- Sea and river goddesses
- Virgin goddesses
- War goddesses
- Water goddesses
- Wisdom goddesses

This gives you a general idea which goddesses we can call upon to show up for us in times of need.

- When we are about to give birth and when we are terrified, we can call on the goddesses of fertility to show up and cuddle our minds.
- When we are confused, we can call on the goddesses of wisdom to ease the confusion and bring us to see the truth in all situations.
- When we've been broken down and our heart is torn apart, we can call on the goddesses of knowledge to guide our minds to where we need them to be.
- When we are feeling anxious and want to settle our minds, we can call on the goddesses of the river so they can show up through turbulent times to help us flow with ease.
- When we are dealing with childhood pain that we want to erase from our hearts so we can live a life full of abundance, we can call on the goddesses of childhood so they can step up and snuggle with us so we feel comfort over the things that have no place in our hearts.
- When we are fighting the forces and we're torn between sex and the moral path, we can call on the goddesses of virginity

to remind us our temple is sacred and our yoni should be cared for with the utmost respect.

- When we are at war within ourselves or fighting the forces of life's events, we can ask the goddesses of war to call a truce so we find our peace within.

- When we need to feel nourished and balanced within, we can call on the goddesses of the earth to whisper in our ear that we must eat more fruits and vegetables so we live life in harmony with our vision.

- When our children are sick and in need of healing, we can call on the goddesses of the earth to direct us to natural medicine that leads to our healing.

- When our relationship is full of chaos, we can call on the goddesses of love to come forth and gently show us patience and understanding toward our partner.

- When we are traveling at night with no protection, we can call on the goddesses of the night to protect us as we journey through life.

- • When we are feeling the effects of karma due to events out of our control, or situations that showed up to lead us to our learning. We can call on the goddesses of time and fate to heal our closure issues that have been thrown in our faces.

- When we aren't feeling well and we need inner healing, but we don't know where to start, we can call on our goddesses of health to show up and help us find our healing.

- When we feel like everything in our sphere has been destroyed and we've given up hope, we can ask our goddesses of destruction to come forth and help us mend the pieces of our shattered heart so we can finally move forward with a bright future.

- When you have talents and you're having a hard time creating something that fuels a fire in your heart, you can call on the goddesses of creation to help ground your mind and focus your attention on the task so you will succeed.

- When you are in the heat of a fire, with no way out, you can call on the goddesses of fire to assist you as you inhale and exhale fresh air that leads to your survival.

Chapter 4

When I was a little girl, I always thought flowers were beautiful. I loved to sit in the sun and plant new seeds and watch them blossom from the sun's nourishment. I realized I loved flowers even more when I would dress up and everything had to match, as I was a true feminine soul. I thought my attire was never complete without a flower in my hair. I had a flower for every occasion. I had every color I could possibly think of. I never realized back then the relationship between me and the flowers were so intimate until I got older and began to explore what it all meant.

As I explored, I realized that we have a lot in relation to flowers. The feminine and flowers both unfold beautifully. The flower and the feminine both go through changes as the season changes. The flower and the feminine both come alive from the sun, and they both need to be replenished by water to feel nourished. And today I will take you on a celestial tour that explains nature and sacred feminism.

For those of you who have read my previous book, Goddess Fly Away, you might have noticed that I am in love with Greek mythology and what it all represents. I began to fit the pieces of this book together when I read the story of Aphrodite and her tears that fell from her face as she was in a marriage that hurt her soul, and how god formed a rose. So I will bring you with me as we unfold, ever so gently, just like the rose.

Chapter 5

Aphrodite: Goddess of the Rose

"So sweet and delicious I become, when I am in bed with the man that I love. I love when the touch of my body brings him delight. I love when the knot of love becomes tied and he unwraps me like Christmas Eve night."

Aphrodite Goddess of love was the goddess who represented love, sensuality, peace, grace, passion, beauty, pleasure, and sexuality. Her symbol is indeed the beautiful rose, so I will use her as our prime example to connect with earth.

Aphrodite was born from the foam of the sea and was called the sea goddess. She was born when Cronus ejaculated into the sea and his little drop landed and created Aphrodite from the foam. Her mysterious birth gives her an air of mystery that she carries with her in her in all that she does.

As the waves swayed, pearls dropped at her feet, making Aphrodite the queen of beauty and luxury. She floated her way to Greece, where she was greeted by the gods, who provided her with attire worthy of her beauty.

Aphrodite's marriage to Hephaestus wasn't a happy one as she was a hopeless romantic, and her husband wasn't. She loved to bathe in the essence of the rose and wore high-heeled shoes, but her husband's lack of interest resulted in her affair with Ares. Aphrodite desired a young man, and his name was Anchises. She was so in love with this man that she decided to become a mortal woman and commit to him fully.

Aphrodite, goddess of love, would shed tears to no end and as God watched her crying, it beckoned upon him to fulfill her heart's longing, so he created a rose to form at her feet to remind her of the beauty she holds within and to show her the beauty of the feminine spirit. Upon placing this rose at her feet, his intention was to make her see the beauty within herself.

He wanted her to see that she could hold herself together the same way as the rose petals. He gave her a cleansed soul, receiving the unfoldment of her feminine soul. Roses are known to bring forth the hiding of beauty and sensitivity. The Rose is our angelic doorways that open our soul to compassion. She steps in and assists us in healing the wounds of our delicate soul. They help us align all our impurities and help us discover that we are woman and vulnerability is okay. Roses give us permission to be a woman. When I was exploring my essential innocence, I discovered that roses stole my heart and brought me back home to myself. They touched me so deeply as they revealed to me who I really am. I heard their whispers as they asked me to say to myself never be ashamed of my sensitivity as that is who I am. The rose in my eyes is a woman's portal to a gentler, more loving and a more beautiful goddess.

Aphrodite's Message

I am the star maiden of the divine lightning bolts that has come to wake you up. Wake you up from the slumber of illusions you've built around yourself. The time is now my daughters, to clear the black cloud to allow the sun to nourish you with its love. Surrender my love and feel the essence of the chapters turn before your very eyes. As you rise from the cusp of the earth I speak. Each page turns, holding a memory of me loving you endlessly.

My darlings, when I was given life I arrived alone. Swept in by the cusp of the sea and alone, I laid there.

I had no mother to wrap her arms around me and say," look at my beautiful daughter." I had no dad, who looked in my eyes and said," that's my beautiful girl." My greeting was the remains of foam that protected me. Sat there by the sea, crying for someone to find me. Eventually the waves swept me away to foreign lands into the arms of people who treated me tenderly. On the rock, I remained seated while steadily crying. While I was crying in the silence of night, a slight wave reached me. It was the fresh wind of the loved ones who treated me tenderly.

Surrendering to the inevitable, I headed for the mountain. I was being taken to foreign lands over the rocky hill, to a soft meadow where the most tender people wait, but I approached cautiously to admire their splendours. My darlings, I came to be accepted through creating loving environments everywhere I went.

I become the homage that was shown love through my actions. It was me, when my sisters came within sight I lifted them up through my gentle whispers and carried all their fears away. My temple was home, a rich and beautiful palace.

It was me, who created a life with my husband and started my own family, so I no longer felt alone. I chased his feeling of protection, because a female goddess living in a world with war needs a man's safety.

I became characterized by many as having relationships that were transient, but that was not who I was. In my defence, I loved him so deeply. My husband Hephaestus, that is. I also needed somebody to be there for me.

My husband hasn't touched me in ten years prior to my acts of momentary pleasure. If he had heard my complaint I would have never felt compelled to engage in such acts.

When I felt Ares close to me my heart would beat just from the mere sound of his voice whispering. All my fears would diminish and my heart felt at ease. It was my temple my loves, that everyone came into to pray. It was my love that sheltered them. All my sister goddesses came to me and I raised the lamp in honour of their fears.

My husband never permitted me to have encounters with other men, but after years of not being touched my body began to desire the touch. I desired a younger man who proved to be a true and gentle lover. After a while, I was unable to restrain myself from making love to him.

You have been freed. Free to love, free to feel and free to understand the ways of the world. My cup of love is offered to those who dare to accept my love. I want you to know, I have never left you even though they want you to think I did. I was the light sprinkling my medicine upon you at birth. I was there with you on your journey. I've watched you cry countless times.

I've seen your fear through the doorways of your soul when you thought nobody was looking. I've watched you struggle and I see your strength. I am the missing piece that your heart has longed for, but you didn't know it was me. Yes, it was me all along riding the waves of the tides when you thought you shall drown. I dusted divine justice upon your head and saved you from yourself. I am the rose who carries the blood that anoints a new beginning, but only for my daughters ready to declare her name.

I Aphrodite gave the rose its character. My daughter, didn't they tell you. It was me laying there wounded at the cusp of the sea. The rose is red, because it was my blood that was wounded and stained it red from my blood. It was me who ran to the sea afraid and the rose allowed me to express myself. My tears were the purity of my heart's longing that I couldn't express unless I went to my divine father. Roses symbolize love, beauty, femininity, expression, and sensuality, because this was who I was before my blood created her. Red is our colour, for red is the blood in which we all were created. The red rose that blooms within your heart is the sheltered cloak of the rose.

This is how we were created. This is our story, so go now and let all men know who you are. Tell them you are powerful and created from pure love. Not only are you the barrier of life, but you rose unfolding your yoni to the most deserving.

Now that you know who you are, I insist that you demand respect. You shall never shrink to the whims of a man who abuses your offering for the satisfaction of his ego. The rose was created with thorns that hurt- such as a woman's voice. Speaking so powerfully, she tears down all walls. She was made fragile to the occasions of her environment. She rises like the sun when she is nurtured and shrinks when her environment shows her no love. I am the Goddess that unravels the mysteries of the universe to the daughters who wish to respect my teachings. The seven petals reveal the true name of the feminine.

I am the deliverance of all that is sacred and true. The oil dusted upon you to awaken your third eye and show you the truth of the world, like the mother of blood who rises from the ashes of the earth. I know every one of your souls, because I have felt them. I have kissed every tear that you have ever shed. Seek me in the darkest depths of your soul and you shall find pure love, for within me is the medicine of the rose.

I am the oil of sweetness that every man falls to his knees and falls in love. If you feel shame of the tale of my being, I shall wear your shame and clothe myself with the silk garments of my eternal petals that unfold. I am the connector of polarities of woman and man, because the rose is the inspiration of the heart. Therefore, I am the empowerment of the heart. Only through searching for the roots of me shall you discover how powerful the feminine really is. It is through trying to dismiss who I am that I shall raise my voice that pricks you. For I am love and the rage that holds the cup below my breast and for him to touch me, he must be deserving.

It is only through finding the root of the cups shall my love pour onto you. Through the remembrance of your divinity, I close this chapter of my heart by offering you the truth of the rose. This truth that was never said to be a truth guides you back into my womb.

Chapter 6

* **Eurydice**

I love to draw forth the literary tradition of the goddess as inspiration in modern fiction. Orpheus music made people fall in love and their hearts would expand. Orpheus was a musician, creating music that touched everyone from the inside out.

Eurydice was drawn to Orpheus's music and felt his voice had put a spell on her as it always drew her in.

Something inexplicable tugged the hearts of the two young people and soon they fell deeply in love, unable to spend a single moment apart. After a while, they decided to get married.

Orpheus fell in love with Eurydice, a woman of unique beauty, both deciding to get married.

However, things would soon change and grief would over power their happiness.

There was one man who was despising Orpheus and desired Eurydice for his own. Aristaeus, had plotted a plan to conquer the beautiful nymph. And there he was, waiting in the bushes for the young couple to pass by. Seeing that the lovers were approaching, he intended to jump on them and kill Orpheus. As the shepherd made his move, Orpheus grabbed Eurydice by the hand and started running pell-mell through the forest.

Eurydice falling deeper in love followed his light and supported him as he walked out the caves of the underworld with him. There was this contract made between Hades and Orpheus. She could follow him, but he must not look back at her prior to leaving the cave or he would loose her. Violating Hades terms of agreement Orpheus looked back and she disappeared In thin air.

Orpheus in disbelief and often not trusting his intuition.

One day as Orpheus was wandering the Forrest she was discovered by a man who was mesmerized by her beauty. That man started to pursue her without hesitation. Eurydice wanted to stay true to her vows and decided to run away from the man. As she ran, she left her husband behind and as she ran he heard her scream. Hearing his wife scream, he runs to her with a desperate attempt to save her, but he had realized she had stepped on a poisonous snake and she laid there lifeless.

As he approached her she was lying there lifeless in the Forest. Orpheus, torn to pieces, dropping to his knees and begins to sing. Orpheus sang his sorrows away over his lost wife's body.

Orpheus wanting to follow her wanted to dip down into the underworld to find the love of his life, but discovered he couldn't enter the underworld twice. He discovered that no mortal has ever entered the underworld and case out alive. Feeling hopefully I'm his own capabilities, he believed I will not die if I dip down under, but I will walk the earth again with my wife by my side. On this journey he begins. Travelling far and wide he makes it to the underworld only to be stopped in his tracks by guards, so he begins to sing a musical that's soothing and the guard falls asleep. Bursting through the doors he asked Hades to set his wife free I need her with me. To become more convincing, he plays his lyre and it sounds so beautifully. Hades felt the love in his heart and agreed to release the beauty. Singing himself the blues, calling on death so he could join jer

Hades asked the guards to release the Eurydice with conditions.

"You may lead Eurydice out, but you will not be able to hear her or touch her. If you do she will automatically be sent back." With excitement Orpheus says yes.

Heartbroken, he started singing love music hoping it would travel to her soul. Singing, music so pretty even the birds would pause to listen in.

Would you travel to the underworld in the name of love?"

Roaming the Earth with his heart hurt.

He sings, to the heavens, bring my wife back. As each day intensifies, tears drop that won't stop.Laying in his own puddle of sorrow he sings to the birds and the bees. Within his secret self, he carved her portrait in the sky and saw nothing, but a beautiful face.

Mumbling to himself he says," I will never stop searching to find you until I have you in my arms." Fearless, I travelled to you, because life is not worth living without you.

Travelling distant lands making a solid commitment to keep moving forward until you are home at last.

❀ Goddess Hestia

I sit at the threshold of the sanctuary, the house of God. As you seek the deeper meaning of my existence you shall discover that I am the spiritual bride and Mother" to all. The maiden pulsating all strength and love. I wear lighter fluid on top of my close like a fragrance.

I tend the holy fire so peacefully- full of delight, with soft oil dripping over from my locks. I invite all to come into my home, come my darlings, as I shall bestow grace upon you.

In the high dwellings of all, both ancients and on earth, through me you shall gain an everlasting abode and the highest honour a woman shall receive.

My heart is the pillar at the entrance of the temple pouring out streams of love. I am the provider of the embers that do not fade.

Today as you become aware of your need to explore my existence my offering is wisdom & warmth. I am the maiden that allows you to see that there is satisfaction in a quiet life.

I, my darlings, was never attached to people, outcomes, possessions, prestige or power, because I felt completeness in myself.

When my feminine values felt forgotten, or dishonored, I remembered my value as I burned the fire that called all into my chambers that reminded me of my contribution to the world.

When there is a need to focus on one matter at a time, or a sense of peace and stillness is necessary I am your guide. My life comparisons and competitiveness are left outside the door for I am inner peace.

My darlings, I did not engage in gossip, as my gift to you would be to listen with a compassionate heart, staying centered in whatever turmoil is happening around me, providing a warm place right by the fire.

I am the keeper of the secret flame that kept all safe and warm. As you enter this space you experience harmony, laughter and safety.

The voices of those who screamed out among the embers that offered peace, often wanted understanding and asked questions like.

* Teach me how to care for my body
* Help me to identify what I am feeling and why.
* Teach me how to ask for what I need without feeling quilts.
* Teach me how to honour my body like a lady.

How do you relate to me, my darlings? I am the goddess who was worshipped as a virgin goddess. I took a vow to celibacy although many men lusted after me. In fact Poseidon and Apollo wanted to marry me, but I declined, because no matter which man I chose it would bring conflict.

I found myself being pursued romantically by Apollo and Neptune. I rejected their advances, however, despite my wishes to remain a virgin Apollo and Neptune continued to pursue me, leading me to appeal to Zeus to intervene. He granted my request to the home.

My darlings, I was a humble goddess who was above the petty politics the world could bring, because I decided not to mingle in it.

If you were to visit Greece on Good Friday you would witness the traditional candle ceremony that is deeply rooted in my memory. They light candles from a central flame at church and carefully bring them home safely. This flame is sacred and connected to me and my love. This candle purifies and cleanses the soul.

The word yoni, if translated, means "vagina." It is also known to be the dedicated temple of a sacred female, a divine passage that leads to the yoni temple of sacredness. Goddess Hestia honored her yoni as it represented her claiming her innocence as she remained pure. The yoni was her sacred symbol, sent for her from the divine feminine. It is sacred because it births babies that the world needs to be full and complete. Our yoni is our contribution to the earth and to be held in the space that allows us to ease in and claim our sexuality as feminine women.

Imagine that your body is the representation of Hestia, the goddess of virginity, in your nakedness. How will you greet this goddess? Imagine yourself being her as a source of beauty and light, standing in front of the most handsome man and holding a flower between your thighs.

Think of yourself as the beautiful and unique goddess Hestia, full of wisdom, compassion, and innocence, being showered with an open arm that stretches as she leans in to say, "Your yoni is connected to your heart." Now imagine the goddess of wisdom, stepping in to reveal your yoni is sacred, before she steps away from the light, as the young man you desire comes forth. As you are overflowing with sexual desire and love, she is full of vulnerable emotions to give. Goddess Hestia is sending you a rose as a symbol of your sacred yoni, so you stand up, cherish her, so you stand up and love her, so you place her as high as the sky, so you respect her for all that she is and all that she's not. Remember you have just received the sacred symbol of the divine feminine. This is your sacred symbol from the heaven to claim your power as a sacred feminine.

Chapter 7

● Gaia

> "I am not breaking apart.
> I am falling
> into place." - Vange Cain

In the time before time I heard a call from the cosmos of such illustrious beauty, and answered the call. Answering the call of divine love opened the doorway for all to see a new land. I go by many names, but in an effort to better connect and to help you understand my energy, I will explain the myriad of forms in which I may appear in your mind on Earth. I give my condolences to anyone who's ever got lost in the false image of me.

I apologize for all the misunderstandings that was placed on my name. There is so much of my past self that you have not come to understand, but if you knew the truth you would love me just the same.

I'm sorry they lied to you about the light in me and the way I rose to give my heart to you. Love caught my eyes from the very first sound of your cry.

All along we've shared this secret language between us and our energy fed off one another. When they pronounced me dead I searched for you only to tell you that I never left you. Please know, night after night my heart lived to forgive.

As we transcend into time we shall weave the dreams that we're once forgotten. I'm so proud that weve held on together and a new memory was born.

As I hunt, I bask in this feeling inside of me to know you. Screaming my wants into thin air you appear and I felt your soul in moments of your every hidden cry.

I knew there would come a time that you would search for me and we would cross the threshold to reunite. I think you were always supposed to know me better than anyone else.

Our loves fated to coverage like some cosmic dance. Coming from various frequencies, even those not from the ancient world are coming together here and now in order to restore the unity of all creations and collapse heaven on earth.

I'm a holy woman. I know what it's like to give love to others without expecting anything in return. I held my tongue long enough to say goodbye— knowing one day we would breathe each other in. We exist to be united for I am the matrix of the ground you walk on.

My soul does not speak human language; I communicate through symbols, metaphors, dreams and magic. Yes, we derived from different corners of the universe sailing admits the sea and I captured you. We met dear ones through the Will of the Creator and according to the divine plan that has been unfolding since the beginning of time. My wisdom has come to set you free. Some of you need freedom in your heart for the truth shall set you free..

You great daughters of mine who were carefully crafted vessels, sturdy and strong, built to withstand the storms of separation to reunite once again. Sorry your under the impression you understood, me, but the truth is—they seduced your mind. Telling you I'm an angry woman and some days I was, but I still loved hard even when my heart was aching. I've spend plenty of time searching for someone to understand me better and then you and my daughters have found me. You became a part of me the moment I laid eyes on you. Wherever you went—I went, because I knew I was part of you.

As I place my heart on the mantle of the earth my heart swings open and I reveal to you that the world watched for me to make one wrong move so they ridicule me. I tell you all that is true, but before I do, please understand that as I bring you out of the shadow of deception my heart was pure love.

I am Gaia the mother never to be ignored, for I was placed on the earth to protect and love all of you.

As I rest at the feet of the Lord I rise to see the light of illumination and I bring this gift of wisdom from the heavens to you.

To those of you who seek to know me- leave your heart as an offering and to you I vow to always walk amongst you. I vow to always lift you up on the mantle of hope and victory for that is where you've always belonged.

As you utter my words to your other sisters you speak the words of truth. As you cross the pathway of the earth you shall find me there waiting with open arms for you.

Please come to understand that I am the golden alchemist that transitions all of life. I give to you the chance to discover who I am.

The time has arrived for the veil to be lifted, show your eyes as the pathway is clear for you to enter into the covenant of love. As you enter dears, you shall discover a gift waiting for you.

I shall bring to you all that I am- which is the vibration of love.

At the feet of the lord I rise to see the light of illumination and I bring this gift from the heavens to you. As you leave your heart as an offering to me I vow to always walk amongst you, to protect and cherish you. I vow to always lift you on the mantle of hope and victory. As you utter my words you speak the words of divine love. As you cross the pathway of the earth you shall find me there waiting to greet you.

I am the golden alchemist that transitions all of life. I give to you the chance to discover who I am to you. The time has arrived for the veil to be lifted leaving a pathway for you to enter into the covenant of love.

As you enter deer ones you shall discover a gift waiting for you.

I was the goddess of the earth—your great mother, the creator of all things. I was the creator of birth and the earth. I was a Powerful goddess who created the earth, and from my fertile womb, all lives began. I am the goddess who used plants to bring harmony, wholeness, and balance within my environment because I knew it was my duty to sustain the earth as that was what I primarily represented.

I brought the beauty to the earth because I knew I was responsible for all things. I dear ones, sprung forth the lilies, the peonies, and the roses to squeeze its medicine onto the gods and goddesses and to provide the essential medicine they need to feel whole, nourished.

My darlings, I think you should know. That I have loved you all so unconditionally embracing you exactly as you are. I paved the way for you to sink your roots into the earth. After all the love I gave, in return, they tried to steal my heart.

Many have tried to dig deep into the most intimate parts of me-leaving my heart there to bleed.

Judged me for the turbulence that was built, because I had to protect myself. They witnessed the tears pour down my face as they turned their backs on my cries.

Yet, as I revealed my story the world became distracted, so they could no longer hear me, feel me, and know me. Treating me as if I was a mere dumping ground. My heart was there soaking up all the pain and my inner screams were so loud it made the heavens cry and pierced the air. I was so tired of not being heard and through it all I still rise to hold you close to my tender aching heart. I hold space for the release of your wounds- I invite you to shed them. Slowly, one by one bit by bit, just let go of them.

Dear Daughters, may you be torn from the shackles life has put on you. I pray that your heart expands wide and the sun beams in and uncovers the layers of pain you've been subjected to. It has been my dying wish to see you return to pristine order and that you find life again.

❀ Our Prayer

I honour the Earth as I walk barefoot. I refuse to carry the sins of others within my heart. I need nature as it is my oxygen.

I am a woman whose love for creativity and wildness sparks my imagination to wonder and roam. I am a woman who sees nature as my medicine to heal the world. I am the woman who squeezes the peony's medicine onto you to brighten your spirit. Gaia was the mother of plenty of children and had the power to birth them without an active father. Gaia is the goddess who says to all those souls searching for a mother or father to gowithin. She says if you don't know your mother or father, she will claim you, and you are forever loved. And I myself had no parents, but we are still so special. We are the children of the divine force that is very strong. I am a woman who believes in right and wrong.

I am a woman who talks to Earth as I write my stories and songs. I am a woman who believes everything can manifest love.

Sage:

When you wake up in the morning and you're wanting to start your day off with love and peace, you embrace your goddess's strength. Call on goddess Gaia, mother of the earth, to sit with you as you light some sage to stimulate your room, as it projects inner growth and well-being. Bathe yourself in appreciation and gratitude for all people and things in your life that Mother Earth has left to you to dwell upon. Breathe in the aroma of nature's natural healing, so you may dwell in acceptance, enlightenment and understanding of your life's experiences.

❀ Say a prayer:

Into this smoke, I release all energy that harms my heart and stops me from flourishing into my fullest potential. Breathe into that beautiful smoke, it will allow me to see clearly amidst the gig. As I exhale and release, it eliminates hurtful thoughts and fears that have been holding me back. Gaia, mother of the Earth, thank you for this beautiful creation that leads to my enlightenment.

Chapter 8

❀ Awaken the Divine Feminine

Today we dive in to embrace the awakening of the divine feminine goddess. The woman who dares to awake from her emotional power to embraces her feminine side. A goddess knows there is more to her than just her intellectual world. She understands that there is something deeper, swimming inside her womb, to be explored. She understands that to deny her feelings is to deny being an intuitive woman.

How can a goddess ever feel love, endure her sensuality, and step into her womanhood without embracing her emotional side? Our emotions are not meant to be turned off. They were given to us to cuddle us and nurture the feminine we are.Yes, we have plenty of feelings. We cry when we watch love movies, our hearts hurt when our children fall, we feel deeply as our grand partners age, and they experience pain, and our hearts open wider and feel even more when we are misunderstood.

We can nurture and honor our hearts as the goddesses have displayed before us. They show us how to persevere and understand our emotions better. They show us through gentle guidance that emotions can be a great expression of who you are or a burden if not checked. Hold your heart in your hands as you cuddle your feelings that display themselves so strong. Breathe in then release your breath and examine how it feels when your heart is pumping out your chest. Show kindness and appreciation, for your heart, because you are loved.

When we cast love, it travels through the air, and the universe responds and gives us air. Casting love is a powerful tool that opens the conscious mind to dream as we manifest our dreams.

❀ Emotional Awakening

Today the goddesses ask you to dive in and embrace the awakening of the divine feminine within the core of your being. This is the woman who dares to awaken from her emotional power so she can embrace her feminine side that's been waiting for her to arrive. This is the day that you will realize that there is more to your overall makeup as a woman than just your intellectual side. The goddesses understand that there is more, swimming inside your womb, to be explored than you know. They want to know how you will ever tap into your womanhood to elevate that part of yourself if you shy away from your feminine side. The goddesses say, "To deny your feelings as an embodied woman is to deny being a feminine woman." How can a goddess step into feeling loved, endure her sensuality, and arrive to meet her emotional power if she won't embrace it? Our emotions weren't given to us to be shut off like a light switch. They were given to us to show up and cuddle and nurture the goddess within us.

Yes, as women, we feel lots of things. Yes, our hearts hurt and our hearts open wider from certain situations. Yes, we feel deeply, but the depth of that deepness was given to us to nurture, love, care, and protect the world. The goddesses before us say, "We must gather in love so we can display our love toward the land." Just like they did in the ancient years, they will show up to hold our hands. They will be with us in whatever forum we need them to be. They will show up to help us persevere and guide us gently to be the goddess we're meant to be. They will show us through a gentle guidance that our emotions are our beautiful expressions of our feminine soul. But as they hold our hearts in their hands, we connect heart-to- heart. This heart-to- heart allows you to experience your feelings deep inside your whirlpool that has been swimming its way to the light. The goddesses say, "Breathe in and hold your breath and then ask yourself, how does it feel to be an embodied woman? How does it feel to carry hurt that you can't release? How does it feel to simply be a woman? How does it feel to open wide to her tears? How does it feel to be misunderstood? Do you feel unloved and untouched? Is your heart bleeding out of love?

How does it feel when you feel your grandmother's pain as an embodied woman? How does it feel to be betrayed by the man of your dreams? How does it feel, in the pit of your stomach, to feel like you're not enough?"

How does it feel to breathe in with calmness and notice the goddesses Yemaya, Aphrodite, Arianrhod, Athena, Diana, Gaia, Luna, and Rhea show up to say it is okay to embrace being a woman? You are surrounded by so much love. No matter who has hurt you, you have experienced. You are the goddess of the land, the birther of all things, and the beauty that the world needs to bring love endlessly.

❀ Awaken from Within

Have you ever found yourself awakening from within, but you never understood what it all represented? I can relate because when I started to open up, I felt this gravity pulling me back. I felt myself more sensitive, more vulnerable, and more aware than ever, and I couldn't place where these feelings came from and why they wouldn't leave me alone.

What if you awaken and become more kindred and more in tuned with humanity to explore becoming more feminine? What if I say we can receive a graceful, divine love that will melt away all our insecurities? This book will offer you an integrated, feminine approach that helps you dive in and discover your own battles that need to unfold and be casted into the divine hands, the resolution to unglue and sit with past hurts. I will help those who are ready to embrace the feminine side in themselves without feeling ashamed. We will explore the self-discovery that reveals the radiant, majestic, and undesirable beauty that lives in the depths of our being, which needs to be explored and felt. We will cuddle with the divine as we feel its support and grace. It is such a beautiful blessing when a goddess can cast love onto the world so fiercely that the world rejoices and sings. Rejoices to the vibrations that seem surreal but full of colors, bright enough to bestow happiness.

Every feminine goddess awakens from within to celebrate the unity of the sacred goddess within.

Chapter 9

❧ Artemis, Step Forth

Goddess Artemis was an independent woman, who never needed a man to make her feel whole and complete. Love never sparked a desire in her to rise like Aphrodite, the goddess of love. Aphrodite was the kind of woman who always wanted to help her man because she had that mother instinct that was instilled deep in her soul. She needed to feel love in order to feel whole and desirable. But nagging a man comes from our inner insecurity—an insecurity that says, "Please give me reassurance." As women, if we feel that things aren't our way, the results will fail, but Artemis had an active conscious which never needed a man's direction to move. She never needed to go within to find her vulnerability and to express love. She knew who she was and never felt sidetracked by others and their competition. She knew she was her own competitor, so she started to find her own race.

Goddess Artemis says, "If there is trust, then there is no doubt!" Artemis never felt the need to doubt her partner because she had no fear that surrounded in trusting him.

She was so preoccupied with her own achievements, so it never presented a concern in her mind. She had this beautiful "moonlight vision" that was active rather than playing the passive role. She was the goddess who protected woman and hovered them like a bear. Aphrodite always had great confusion in her mind, and she always needed reassurance in regard to love. She needed to know if a man was in love with her or someone else. She always second-guessed what he said, she wanted to put together the pieces behind his actions. Aphrodite always wanted men to fulfill their promises. Artemis never second guessed a man because she knew it wouldn't make him feel inclined to do more. She knew he didn't like that kind of relationship with his mother, so he wouldn't like it from her. A woman who can hold the intent to find harmony with her soul's calling is as beautiful as a river that's flowing. When she flows, she finds her still quietness with ease.

Chapter 10

❀ Goddess Yemeya

Celestial blessings my dear loves, I am Vange, here as a representation of goddess Yemeya. I am the founder of The Queens Mansion Academy and I bring to you a channeled message from our beloved goddess Yemeya. I asked her to speak through me and deliver this message of love and truth to you right here and right now. I come to you with a wide open heart and a message of pure unconditional love.

❀ Message From Yemeya

Please let me reveal that I live in your presence. Let me make it clear that I have never left you. My remains left, but my image always stayed. My daughters let me tell you something. Your ancestors are the ones who brought you here and fought for you to stay, so you could remain on earth and spread your light.

You have always been part of the plan and even though you may endure much darkness there cannot be light without darkness. There is beauty in the dark. Your seed began in my womb that is of a dark place and it created daughters of divine love. The chaotic waters of the unknown created pure radiant beauty. As you come to understand me better, please know that it is your mission to speak through me. I ask that you be the divine tongue that represents my name.

Let me reveal that you are the new guardians left here to walk in my image and as you open the garden to your soul you shall find Eden who asks you to plant only seeds of love. As you connect with the soil you intertwine with the web of the goddess. You are the clay molded by my resemblance to walk for me on this earth. Therefore, it is crucial that you hold humility and be humble in the name of your ancestors

Today, I bring to you this message to open your consciousness and to show you what I represent.

I, the queen of the seven seas, freed so many.. As I reveal my story it will become apparent that in my moments of existence I had special abilities with water and I worked tiredly to explore my given gifts and free the people from the darkness of ignorance and bring them into the light of illumination and love.

There was a false matrix on earth and that was not the glimpse of hope.

The world was subjected to spiritual starvation and I was the body of hope that carried all of you to a land of safety.

My first introduction to the world was through the seashell that was raised high to honor my beautiful voice so that I would never be forgotten.

Every time you pass by an ocean and embrace its gentle breeze or rest your eyes on a beautiful seashell, we must rise and listen for her whispers of the unseen.

I am the queen who clears the black clouds to allow the light of the sun to find its way to you.

I place my heart on the mantle of God's portal and I reveal who I am and therefore a new memory is born. I have always been the honoured one. The mother to all.

I first became aware of you the day you took your first breath. When the creator separated us that was the moment I became aware that I needed to free you. The hearts of the angels cried as they witnessed me walking to the east, walking to the west, scoping the north and the south so that I could find you. I tirelessly carried you in my heart and I never let you go.

I searched the sea doing everything I could to find you and when I did I carried you within my arms to safety once again. Yes, I am the bright evening star that you shall follow into the chambers of freedom for I can be trusted.

I am the queen of the ocean who reveals the mysteries of purity.

I am love and I must reveal that I swam with my cup of love in my arms, that I offered only to those who wish to learn the mystifying stories of my being. I am the midwife who bears her labour pains. I am strong and I am fear. The one disgraced and shamed for who I was and I was casted out of the earth. I was made to feel ashamed only for being who I was.

I was looked down upon as an evil witch, but the truth is I saved many. I am compassionate yet they silenced my name during their councils, but here I am. I reappear and I 'll speak the truth to all of you. I was the one who was hated everywhere and loved everywhere.

To be frank, those who hated me carried ignorance in their hearts. I am the one whose ashes was scattered across the ocean breeze and yet so many don't even know they are stepping upon the seeds of my fertile ground.

I am the wise lady cloaked in the purity of the angels who sent me to save you. The woman who hands you the sword of truth that teaches you balance and justice. I prepared you to fight back as I sheltered you with the armour of knowledge and truth. It is I, here to remind you of who you are dear ones and it is through this understanding that you find your home. Home is in the arms of the divine mother who bathed you, clothed you, fed you and kept you safe from harm. I carried you in my nest of love to be here to represent the goddess that we all are today.

As you travel back home to me it becomes apparent that I have always journeyed into this life with you. As your heart beats with mine oh warrior goddess- please take the tools I have given to you and spread your net wide. 'Do not' look back even in times of fear for I promise I shall never leave you. I died for this word and you must uphold my name and free me from the image the world createdb of me, because that vision was never who I am.

My darlings, do not swim against the tides of my love or detour in the opposite direction as I am not to be feared. I am your safety. My dear sweet daughters, don't you see that paradise is yours because of the sacrifices I have made before you arrived. It was me, who crushed the wicket with my tail to set you free.

I have always been with you. I watched your every struggle dear ones. I saw the enemy snatch up your soul and I witnessed you fight back, but you felt like you lost the battle, so you gave up.

I am here to tell you that the battle has just begun and you shall come to have a clear mind as the cataracts are lifted from your eyes—as before this very moment your vision has not been clear, but I am here to lift the smog in order to navigate you in the right direction. Now that you know me, go and spread the word about me. Tell them, all the people, that I am the honoured one and the scorned one.

Please daughters understand that I am here to serve humanity and to save those who have been taken for granted. Call me the seven wonders that unravels the mysteries of the universe.

I am the seven petaled rose that rises to wipe the tears from your very eyes as I know who all of you are.

I am here to help you discover rest for the battle ground you have been on made you see the world from a dark point of view. If you are shameful of anything at all I shall wear your shame with the cloak of my love and sprinkle you with the water that heals- the water which is the splendour of my pureness..I am the queen who spirals my way across the sea grabbing those who are drowning and lifting your head above the waters you fear.

My darlings, please know. That when the temple meets the sky you'll come to understand heaven on earth and see that immortals merge mortals. Therefore, I live forever; never dying. I am the voice who's voice echoes across the lands, because what I speak is powerful.

I am war and I am peace. They attacked me for my weakness and judged me for my power. I am the one who so many learned from. It is me who reappeared when you hid yourself from shame and fear, I showed up as your guiding strength carrying you into the abyss of my love. I peace and therefore water was given to me. I am the gushing over flow that can't be stopped and my powers were never to be buried behind the image of shame for I am yemaya and I ahad so much to offer the world.

If you were to enter the house of worship you would see my name written on the stone door of the temple. If you listen for me dear ones, you shall hear me sing to you and whisper the truth as you walk upon the cusp of the sea.

It is there in that moment that I reveal a truth to you. It is the melody of my voice that sets you free from all your transgressions. Please know, that time is fleeting and it waits for no one, so burn the illusions that held you captive. Free your mind dear one, for I Yemeya is here to serve you the truth and I walk with you on this journey.

As you search for the core of me; then and only then will your heart be set free. Those who left their heart as an offering to me I shall find you and bring you to safer lands.

❀ Letter To Yemeya

Oh Yemaya, Goddess of the Sea,
With utmost respect, I bow before you the queen.
Admiring the power, the energy put forth to save those who were in need. I have the ability to provide safety for you when fear feels like the only possibility.

Can you hear the sweet whispers placed upon the sacred healing waters that purify you?
I am coming, going and resting. The in between, who's becoming part of every breath of yours that beats.

❀ Goddess Yemaya, Step Forth

We ask for your prayers today because some of us are having a hard time birthing the blessing that womanhood brings. So we ask for your blessings to protect, care, love, and shelter our fragile wombs. Goddess Yemaya, we ask you to place your hand on our stomachs and insert your potent power inside our wombs that need your love so we receive your inspiration and strength.

I pray as we conceive and as our fertile wombs produce the seeds of new birth that you show up to hold our hands through this trying time called labor. Lead us to your altar of fertility and strength. Bring us to the sea so we find our courage to conceive.Sit us under your crescent moon so we can connect with your loving blessing and guidance.We are standing at the ocean, looking at the pretty tide, as we receive the blessings from your healing water. We sit as it pushes its way to the shore to caress our toes. We feel the healing water splash upon ours womb and heal us from within. We are here waiting for your love, compassion, and blessing to hug us. We are here to feel the beauty of nature and the joy of motherhood.

We are full of so much gratitude for the blessings that you bring.

❀ Thank you, Goddess Yemaya.

We close our eyes as we inhale and exhale the beauty of your present moment and as we connect with the tides without a sound.

Write down how goddess Yemaya, goddess of the earth, makes you feel as you step forth with nature and the ocean's sweet breeze. How does it feel to be touched with blessings?

Say to yourself in secrecy: "Goddess Yemaya, step forth and allow me to feel your presence. Bless my heart so I glow with ease and allow anxiety to move its way outside my body. Allow me to find balance, tolerance, and understanding in all things. Today we hold our sea shell close to our hearts, under the crescent moon, in memory of your good contributions to those looking to be free. As we commend our fears upon you, we walk with our sea shell as we journey to the ocean to visit you." If we allow our soul to flow, in essence, to the river, we will live in harmony, we will find balance, and we will receive love.

Chapter 11

● **Goddess Arianrhod.**

"A lie told,
is enough to have
a woman doubting
every word you
ever spoke."

She was the earth mother below our feet that healed karmic defeat. She was the goddess who weaved her willpower to free us from karmic fate. She is the goddess who ruled her domain as the goddess of balance, love, and good faith. She was another one of our goddesses who represented being a virgin, as she felt complete from just being by herself and never needing a man as a safety net. She loved her body and the exploration of her sexuality. She believed many women looked for this pleasure from a man, but she believed it's a beautiful portal that leads to her journey to the feminine yoni. She had the power to spin and weave the wheel of life with her bare hands. She was the tapestry of life.

Goddess Arianrhod was in love with birch trees as they represented new beginnings and fresh starts. She loved to float in the sea as it brought forth beauty, peace, and stillness she needed. In times of sadness, she looked at the stars and casted her wish upon them as they reached the land.

The moon goddess is the primal life force that leads to divine feminine power. Today we visit this beautiful goddess, as we embrace her powerful shifts, to unglue us from bad, energetic imprints of karmic energy that have been weighing our hearts down. Many of the actions we've experienced in our past lives lead to a life of agony. We must free ourselves of this agony so we discover the beauty that life has for us. So we look at karma in the face as poverty, setbacks, cruelty, and sufferings ease their way out of our lives. When we're facing hardships that are weighing us down and the black cloud overshadows the light before us, we call on goddess Arianrhod to visit us and bring her healing powers to heal patterns that enslave us. She stands over us in the morning with bright eyes as she reveals, "It's all over, girlfriend, and I'm here to soothe you from your worry and anxiety. All you need to do it take my hand."

❀ Goddess Arianrhod, Step Forth

Goddess Arianrhod, we call on your loving presence to clear all karmic influences that stand in our way. We ask that you send the healing power to cure our hearts from within.Stand with us as we journey through this sacred tour that leads to our enlightenment. When karma has made a root inside our hearts, guide to the gates of freedom. Guide us to the goddess within so we shine so brightly just like the highest star. Awaken the power points inside our soul that have been sleeping for far too long. Show us how to flow in accordance to the divine feminine's essence.Allow the healing powers to take source within so it purifies our soul to a beautiful awakening. Balance our chakras so it directs us to go within and to us.

Chapter 12

● **Athena, the Female Warrior**

Athena was the goddess of wisdom and war. She was fierce and brave during the wars. She never backed down from opposition. Athena held within elegance and beauty that left an imprint that could never be erased. She was called upon in many situations as her input was respected and admired by all the gods and goddesses. She was honored as a mediator in situations because of her sharp intellect and wisdom. I call upon goddess Athena today to participate in directing the goddesses to soothe our inner warrior, so we can let our guards down. She is here today because she has noticed the warrior in you. She hears your cry loud and clear, so I'm here to hold you through your beautiful healing. She understands you've never let your guard down because you've been hurt in the past. She doesn't want you to be embarrassed. She wants you to embrace your goddess's light, and if something happens, she will show up to gently guide you to the right place. Athena and I both know this woman you have become because we too have endured the same pain. She is you and I and so many other women, who hide behind what really is. Athena and I understand the fear that surrounds stepping into that goddess stance; it's that feeling of weakness that takes over you without your warrior sword.

Goddess Athena says it's okay to put down your sword and pick up a lily instead so you can unfold like a true feminine soul, full of beauty, full of class, full of sensitivity, full of blossoms, full of roots, full of openings, full of color, full of life, and full of beauty. She is in need of nourishment, she is in need of tender love and care, she is in need of protection and she needs a life force and a reason to keep on loving, giving, caring, nurturing, not only herself but the others around her too. As Mother Earth, you are the giver of life forces and beautiful energy, and when we give love, we contribute to the earth's core in a loving way. It is our job to settle suffering and nurture the land, and we can't do this with a sword in our hands. Once you step into your truth and allow the resentment, anger, hurt, and betrayal to fly away in the sky, you start to feel yourself coming back to life. So Athena asks, "Will you join her to contribute love to the land, to nurture the trees, and to love the earth? We become a warrior from many things.

You might be that little girl who grew up without a daddy, and you never learned how to relate to a man. You might be that little girl who got raped, and now you guard your body, so no one ever takes advantage of your sacred temple again. Maybe you where mentally abused and know you have flashbacks playing over and over in your head. Some little girls grow up with a mother like me, who does not understand how to display love, for her way of loving me was giving me material things. That little girl carried all that hurt and pain into the battle world, and it stopped her from allowing others in. When I step into my own imagine, of what it feels like to be a warrior woman with a sword. I see so much love hidden behind a fake mask. I see a woman who's too tired to stand. I see a woman broken but still alive. I see a beautiful you, ready to bloom. I see you and me, ready to love and ready to call it truce. I see a woman whose tears are just like goddess Yemaya, who traveled the ocean alongside victims of slavery to protect them. Can they too put their swords down? But as we wipe away the tears, we can finally see that we must surrender to experience the awakening that goddess Athena brings. When we are ready, goddess Athena invites us to join her in the celebration to explore the beautiful transformation of letting our guard down and allowing the goddess's light to shine free.

Chapter 13

❀ **Goddess Diana**

"I am not breaking apart.
I am falling into place."
- Vange Cain

Diana was the goddess of the hunt and wildness. She was the goddess who stood up for women's rights and their freedom. Diana was very attuned to the heartbeat of the wild. She found herself out of balance if she wasn't in harmony with nature.

The birch trees held a special place with goddess Diana's heart because of its love and light. She was infatuated with their fragile appearance, and it made Diana wanted to care for them. She connected with the birch trees because she felt that they both found comfort in the places others refused to find serenity. Goddess Diana was also the goddess of childbirth, but since we've already discussed the roles of a goddess of childbirth, I think I will enlighten you as I open your awareness to the goddess of the hunt and her beautiful attributes. Diana was the goddess honored for many centuries as the goddess of the hunt and then got honoured as a lunar goddess. Diana was in love with wildlife and the excitement it brings. She never went anywhere without her bow as she was always ready to hunt. She was a beautiful goddess always surrounded by animals.

❀ Goddess Diana, Step Forth

As we pay homepage, we create an altar in honor of your existence, so we can meditate and be in your presence. This altar is full love. We've found a birch tree, and it is surrounded with all the animals you love. You are the lady of the wild and goddess of the hunt. Bring forth your survival skills to us. Make room for us to bathe with you in water wells with nature as you comfort us.

❀ Divine Witnessing

This book's substance is all about casting love into the universe, so it projects back onto us. We reach for the divine's flow so we too can live a life of ease. Know that we've gained our wisdom and got to understand ourselves, and now it's time to start manifesting our dreams. It's time to step forth in love if we are truly ready. The divine is going to be the witness of our transformation into subtle and honest beings as we fall in love and allow ourselves to melt and open from his masculine arms, comforting us, keeping us safe, and projecting a strength that only a masculine can portray. As you experience the still, quiet presence, Aphrodite stands and rises to watch you merge slowly into the awareness that is beautifully designed for you from her. She fills you up with faithfulness and a commitment that is rooted deep in your soul. For those of you who have been bruised but not broken and feeling sceptical about love, Aphrodite says, "You are ready, girlfriend. Dive in and take a chance on the universal essence."As we look closer, Artemis will see for she is our granter of wishes, inspiration, and beautiful dreams, a time that says it is okay to awaken to your spiritual aspirations because they will materialize.

❀ The Goddess Insists

Aphrodite insists that you allow love to find its way inside your heart to merge with trust and to allow your wisdom to shine by trusting in yourself enough to know that your heart does not lie and it does guide you to the truth. It is time to stop being led by your ego and love will show up and cuddle you. Close your eyes and call upon Aphrodite, goddess of love, to show up and present love inside your heart. Call on goddess Artemis to show up and merge blessings upon your deepest wishes. Ask for a divine intervention, so you can come into alignment with your masculine and feminine energies that reside deep within. Ask that your feminine energies come into sight with your authentic self.

Now go grab your god box of secrecy and find a quiet place to connect with our beautiful goddess figures. Lift the lid and feel the presence of the goddesses, sitting over you, stroking your hair, cuddling you, and holding your hand, as they guide you through the gates of love's blessings. Meditate on these feelings of love: union, marriage, family, and all the qualities you desire in a man. Now grab your sage and inhale your dreams into the smoke. As you create your sister circle with the goddesses, who love you so much, repeat after me.

May this sage take root, and as it grows, allow me to grow too. May I blossom tall and strong just like the buds of this beautiful sage.

As the sage burns, allow me to clear my chakras, so I receive love. Now hold the sage and ask that love take root and resides within you. Close your eyes and center yourself by taking a few long deep breaths.

Imagine roots connecting deep down into the earth grounding yourself. The sage is going to do the cleansing, but set an intention for what you would like to get out of each session. Are you using sage to heal, to grow, to clear your mind, to invite in new experiences, or more abundance? Set the intention.

Chapter 14

❋ Luna

Welcome my darlings to the world of Luna. I am the Roman ancient goddess who represented the moon. I am the reflection you see as you gazed at the crescent moon. I am the one who rides my horse wearing a crown as I make an entrance. I my dears gave blessings to all as they traveled overseas. I was the soft, shimmering light of the moon that reflected upon us while bringing to the surface our loving emotions that could leave us feeling enchanted and whole as a being.

Today we ask goddess Luna to shine her light upon our dark places that need her light and love and to introduce us to her gazing reflection that highlights a time of rest. I am that beautiful goddess who was most often riding a chariot which represented victory and completion. I was the goddess who made reality clear to those who trusted in me. She rose and initiated flares with enlightenment as psychic awareness became fierce and powerful. I cuddle your fears as you dream. In fact, Hera understood my great abilities and came to me in confidence, explaining to me that she had a dream and wanted to know what it meant. She revealed to me that she had dreamed that her husband Zeus was having an affair with another goddess and she wanted to understand her dream.

Luna revealed that it indicated her fear of being abandoned. She stated that Hera had a heightened desire to have someone there for her. She told her that she was feeling unworthy of his love and didn't feel within herself that she measured up to be the kind of woman he desired because his infidelity led to second-guess her abilities as a woman. Hera revealed to Luna in shame that she wished her husband had the courage to fight off the desires of the women who threw themselves at him. She said it made her feel humiliated and that the most priceless gift her husband could ever give her would be to have the courage to honor their sacred union.

Luna understood the pain and told Hera that in order for her to feel nourished and worthy she must rise to the divine feminine and allow her to be part of her. The divine lifts us up and carries us to the arms of unconditional love that bypasses all our pain, insecurities, and fears that bind Hera, leaving her feeling unworthy.

Where did Hera begin to pick up the pieces that fell upon the ground? She started by grabbing her goddess box of secrets to whisper and reveal her disappointment. Hera felt disappointed because I expected a love from my husband that I didn't believe I could find within my feminine being.I feel disappointed because I yearned for a structured family life that I didn't believe I could create for myself, so I looked to him to find happiness within. I stayed single because my self-esteem was so low. I thought no one else would want me. The goddesses say we are not to blame for other people's actions. She says, "it's time to claim our delicious body." Luna says we are not to blame for other people's actions. She says, "It's time to claim our temples.

Chapter 15

> "As I fall in love
> With the goddess, I also
> Fall in love with myself.'"

Goddess Rhea was the daughter of goddess Gaia, the mother who ruled the earth and the heavens. Goddess Gaia was able to birth new creations and bring everything to light. As Rhea watched her mother rule the earth, she learned rituals of how to hold the earth in its delicate place. She was our goddess of flow, ease, and generation. Rhea was given the name "mother of the goddesses" to honor her birthing the Olympians. Rhea was the goddess who was responsible for the way life flowed in the kingdom. She made sure women's menstrual cycles flowed with ease to eliminate pain and suffering. She was responsible for birthing how the water flowed. She was responsible for the milk that nourished the people. Goddess Rhea represented the swan because of her gentleness and peaceful persona.

Rhea and Cronus had plenty of children together, but every time Rhea got to glance at their cute little babies' previous little faces, Cronus would swallow them out of jealousy— the fear that they would overpower him. He saw the happiness in her eyes when she held her babies. He saw the love that was given, and he became jealous and began to feel fear that he would lose power over the woman of his life. After her sixth child, Rhea went to her mother Gaia, the goddess of Earth, to take her son Zeus because she was fearful of losing him. Her mother understood what it felt like to lose a child, so she agreed to take Zeus and hid him so he would be safe. Goddess Gaia then took Zeus to a hidden cave underground of Mount Olympus. Rhea then went to her husband and have him a stone wrapped up in cloth as a representation of their new baby boy, and without hesitation, Cronus swallowed it without even looking at it. He never knew that his baby boy was still alive.

Hi, my name is Rhea, goddess of love, ease, and flow, and this is what's on my mind.

- Why did my husband swallow his own children?
- Why did he think I'd love him any less because a new baby was born? Because I am a woman of love and compassion, I don't understand why he wouldn't want to see his children grow.
- I've lived a life full of sadness that I can't overcome as I see visions of my babies looking in my eyes. I want to feed them, hold them, love them, and never let them, out of my sight.
- All I ever wanted to do was create a memory book full of you and me, but your daddy took that from me.I went to my mother and father to protect my baby from harm, because I refused to let anyone harm my babies. If you have children, protect them and keep them safe from harm because this is the goddess's way.

Goddess Rhea's Gift

"I am perfect just as I am."

Goddess Rhea is sending a swan your way because she carries within herself their healing essence. This swan is being sent to you so you collide your presence with hers. She needs you just as much as you need her, which is why she's showing up today. She is sending you still divine healing and an act of love with beautiful energies so you can unfold like the beautiful swan.

She sends you out into the still, quiet water so you remain calm as you drift out into the sea, where the goddesses and the swans will meet you with love and devotion. The swans will smile because they are surrounded by this soft, golden glow that is full of the healing energies that you need to never ever give up on your possibilities or dreams. As you enter the sea, so much love is waiting for you to unfold.

Goddess Rhea says, "I know what it feels like to fight for freedom because I hid my son in a cave to keep him safe from harm. I know what it feels like to want freedom, but you don't know where to begin. Today is the beginning of a new journey for us. It can begin as we walk with the earth or endure the beauty of the sea. Goddess, I've been sent so you will feel like you're living heaven on earth.

"Last night, I lay awake by the sea, listening to the swans sing so beautifully. In their songs, I heard my babies cry, 'Mommy, why didn't you save us?' I just lay there with no response, dwelling in my own sorrows until I saw that glimpse of sunlight shining on my body

"In a speechless attempt to answer my babies, the swans drifted over, holding them smugly under their wings, and I saw my babies happy, smiling very gracefully."This morning, I went to goddess Luna and told her I had a dream that seemed so real, and I wanted an understanding of what it all meant. She revealed she had a message to relay to me, but it came as a dream. She said the dream represented freedom of the mind, stillness, elegance, and beauty. She said we would find love and peace in the most effortless way. We must surrender and flow with the still, quiet moments that are calling us into their existence. We must let go and allow the process of knowing to transpire into something bigger than our being."

The swans, which drifted over to us in silence, tell us that we are being guided to a land full of purity and hope. The goddess Yemaya says she has traveled distant lands with the swan intentionally so she can witness our healing and watch us transform beautifully. She's aware that the golden glow that the swan is carrying with her is given from the divine. The swan says, "Beloved, it is time to let go of the pain you've been feeling." The swan's gentle sway sends these vibrations that send the goddess to a place of peace."My golden glow is your light—your light to wisdom and the light that carries all your pain. There is resistance in letting go, so please follow me as we drift to a distant land. "I've shown up to teach you stillness so you can quiet your mind. We've weathered the storm and what didn't kill you sure did make you stronger. I'm here, beloved, to show you your reflection in my light because this is how the goddesses see you. You are a daughter, sister, mother, aunt, grandmother, and cousin in resemblance of this beautiful light. Your heart is free loving in a contained world.

"Goddess Rhea is waiting for you. She wants your permission to step in and guide you to the light. She wants your permission to step in and lead you to freedom. Goddess Yemaya swam the longest detour through some hectic weather so you find your healing. The universe is calling you. Are you ready to drift into the celestial sea of love and purity?"

Chapter 16

🌸 **Daughter Of Gaia**

"I am loved by the queens
of the universe."

Celestial blessings my darlings and welcome. Today as I travel inward I send you a message from mother Gaia who loves you so much.

I am rising cloaked in the juice of the red rose and I have been birthed full of life's mysteries. Crowned with the consolations of ancient love, I am, the queen of the earth who has become the ladder to your soul shall you decide to climb inside my walls of nurturing love. I have risen, pushed my way through the dirt to see you free yourself, so I can walk among you.

As I co-create with my Heavenly Father above we shall set you free. The lining of my womb is the gateway to freedom and the only thing denying your entry is the belief that you don't belong as entry is always available to you. It was my choice, my sacrifice to walk beside you keeping you safe and it may feel as if I am not beside you, but I am. My beautiful children, we are now facing the times of intense heartbreak, both swirling around me, and with yourselves. The world needs your forgiveness, not just for others, but also yourself. These are the times to go deep within. Can you do this for me?" Can you go deep within and heal your inner wounds from your lost love?" My love is your bandaid that covers the open wounds that you carry around with you.

Please call on me, your Mother, to hold you in your fragile emotional state of pain, so that you can release that sorrow, that brokenness that divides you from your heart. The dark, corners within you that are so yearning to be loved up, We are all surrounded by love. I think an important question is, can we receive that love and believe that it is ours unconditionally? I am happy when my children reveal to me that they are ready to be loved, not covered in shame and fear. Often we struggle with feeling unworthy or undeserving and don't allow ourselves to be loved as fully as it is available, particularly from the Divine.

Despite how much you guard your heart I see you wanting love, so I show up to assist you my darling. You my special one, born to create the myriad beautiful forms into which Spirit pours out love. Each new day life offers a new beginning that opens your eyes and allows you to stand face to face with me and gaze into my gentle eyes. My heart reaches out to you, loving you and celebrating you just as you are. If you are in a hard place right now, it is time to come home, because mother Gaia's love, is not withheld regardless the circumstances, because a mothers love is unconditional. Always and forever, her heart and arms are open to you. She will not force you to come into her embrace but she feels comfortable when you do.

If you give her the opportunity she will wrap you in a tender hug that will never end. I know it may take some time for you to arrive at this place of trusting, but I am patient and kind and understanding. I know that life has knocked you down, but you can ask for help from the Divine Realm and it will be given freely. While you slept, I whispered words of love, encouragement and guidance in your ear while you were asleep and as you my words slip into your conscious mind you slowed down,and took some moments to listen. Together we can restore the earth to its natural beauty and abundance. Let us do this together with joy and togetherness.

Do you live to understand the mysteries? If so, you have found your rightful place. Does your soul feel nourished in the soil of my love? Can you hear nature's prayer for your divine communion?

❀ Dear Mother Gaia

Mother Gaia, my voice may be soft, I may be very small: but I am still strong. As we shift our consciousness may we offer you, reciprocated love. We as woman stand tall and strong. May we create the best life for all. Today, we show up as the vessel in the image of the goddess, she who holds all love and light inside. The mysteries of her love and her power have been sheltered from you. As we dive deep into the cave of our hearts, our divine mother nudges us and says," "Don't give up." She asks us to give our past fears to her. She will hold on to them until we are ready to face them. She asks us to slowly let go and don't allow worry and fear to take over our warm embrace. She is offering you love in exchange for you heart. You're safe as she would never let you go should you fall.

Sister, stand tall and be seen.
Shed love onto the earth freely.
Serve the world through your loving gifts
Right now, you are needed more then you can see.
Free yourself, because fear is not your friend.
Let go.
It is time to love my dear.

* Mother Gaia

My daughters, your being has cleansed us all, transmuted the debris we've held within, allowed us to sink our roots into fertile ground and as we dig deep we find ourselves. The root that displays our wholeness and need to love and be loved. We have dug deep into your most intimate caverns of your being without even knowing you were there. Without so much as a thank you for always being there.

In a time before time I heard a call from the cosmos. I saw illustrated beauty where the birds began to sing. I listened carefully to each song. I felt at ease in nature, but my mind couldn't comprehend why. It was the divine feminine searching the corners for peace. Then she opened her eyes to her mother and she was right there all along right with me. I was part of something amazing as we birthed a new beginning. All I felt was love.

❀ **Before the day starts**

I Know you've heard the call within, you've even felt something pulling on your heart strings and tried to distinguish what it is. You know that from the well of our chalice your womb knows who you really are. She knows your ancient feminine power that lives on. She awakes my loves; she claims extended love and spreads it far and wide. She rises with love encoded in her blood, She knows, she has a unique soul contract to fill and rises to the activation of the power she draws from inside. Inanna is rising my loves. She rises cloaked in the silk red garnets of all of life's creation. She says," bow down to me for I am the gatekeeper of mysteries and wisdom untold...

Do you hear me speak to you dear ones?

Should you dare to look inside the secrets of the red doors where I reside, than, and only then will you see me waiting for you.

My eyes of love are fixed on you and I see the real you through all your pain; I see you through the joy you try to contain. I see everything and It is my sacrifice to walk among you, not because I am high and mighty, but because I love you and I stand by humanity.. I to as a child of God have free will and rights and this path is what I choose.

I called my father forth and asked for love and peace to assist him here on this journey. Yes dear ones, I asked to flow wild with the waters so I can create my fire that is of passion that burns for all of you. I my loves, have felt the chapters of divine life rising before you and as each page is turned a new you is birthed. I left a story for you, yes, I earned my respect, I demand to be adored by you for I have sacrificed for thousands of years to nurture you and protect you and show you the gateway to wisdom.. The lining of my womb cradles you and protects you from harm.

❀ Daughter Of Venus

Venus the Goddess of love has asked me to carry a message of truth to you today. She asked that you bring back the divine feminine in you who has been lost searching and trying to find her way home. She has asked that you unveil the love that is encoded in your heart and to rise up my dear one to conquer all illusions and fear. You are asked to look within to discover the open gardens of your heart and follow the authority that is being given to you for the world awaits to plant your seeds of intention. Today, sweet one, I ask you to defend your ancestors and carry their codes of love to dry earth. I ask that you never deny me and to always defend my name for I am mother of the earth who's protected you for thousands of years and I have lived on and left an image of me that is supposed to be engraved in you, so you can walk in my image. As you come to recognize me you come to know yourself and dwell in inner peace and rest.

There are so many who don't understand that I live inside the matrix of Jesus Christ yet many have always denied that I exist, but that does not mean you need to strip my existence from you for I love you and regardless of who can accept this truth or not I am your mother sent to nurture you. I am the womb pulled from the rib of man to nurture you. It is my breast that feeds you. It is my love that leads without command,but comes to you in a nurturing way, to love you, protect you and show you the way. As I carry the message of God you come to see that we are all one walking in the imagination of the all mighty. Remember my loves, that I the gatekeeper of love understands that love conquers all things and that fear is an illusion that isn't real. Fear is a tool used to manipulate you, control you and push you away from your truth of universal love. Every time you accept this fear you, become further from me, the mother, the gatekeeper of love herself.

Daughters of Aphrodite listen to me, do you hear me call out your name? I ask that you remove your veils as its blinding what you can see. It is time for you to know the truth. My collection of tears is accompanied by the man who forgot to cherish me and as I addressed my spiritual quest the water swayed over and cleansed me. I had to release my sorrow somehow, so I picked the petals off the Rose and weaped and pressed my pain into the Rose—gently placing each petal on the water to merge with my tears. Sensations cascade throughout my entire body. Tears come freely, as they land--each one becomes a promise from God. Lying to myself saying," I would never choose this," but the truth is I did. In the moments I asked for new love. It was the tears that mended me back together. I often talked to God, because I doubted anyone would understand and when I'm by the rock I am a island all by myself. I felt it. People talking about me behind my back. I am the Goddess of love, because I am soft. I am vulnerable. I am gentle. I am sensitive. I must admit, I got so tired of hearing I'm weak, because my heart felt so much. Walked with a shield on my heart until one day I had enough. Representing the Rose my feelings came like waves, I taste saltwater and swallow bits of the ocean in my tears. In truth, softness is what makes me so beautiful and powerful. My strength derives from the gushing water of my feelings.

I stomped my feet down and the sea moaned wildly in response. I heard thunder and the sky ripped itself open and produced the rain. You see, I did not suppress my sexiness, for between my thighs lays the Rose. I was boldly unashamed, wholly unapologetic for I did fall in love with someone other than my husband. I would cry to be a free. to be heard In moments when my heart was in pain. I felt the regret, the shame, the loneliness, but I did not judge myself— for I am human.

I was the truth. I guess my darlings, I was made for these depths. Emotions are rivers. My heart roars the petals that prick so harshly. I peeled away my heart and only tears remained and Rose petals revealed my strength.

Come to me my dear.
I'm waiting for you.
Waiting to reveal all the mysteries of life to you. Don't be afraid for I am the light not the dark. I am love.
I am the truth.
And I am here on earth to serve you.
I am here to protect you.
I am the goddess who rose from the waves of foam to greet you.
I have arrived to show you the true light of the world. I died yes, I died to God and came to you as his servant.

Chapter 17

❀ **Lilith**

> "Love sets me free.
> I am married to me
> I am the voice I desire to live."

As we uncover the cultural contexts of Lilith, we come to see that she represents chaos and destruction- a reflection and a mirror to another way of carrying ourselves as a woman. As I bring myself on a journey inside myself I sit and I write. Now that we are all here together, what do we talk about? Let's talk about you being a radiant being full of light and love. Let's call Mother Earth the nurturer of our needs.

Dear Mother Earth, thank you for showing me the true goddess in me. Thank you for walking beside me peacefully. You know I can be selfish, impatient, and out of control. You know I blow the whistle. You know I'm irrational and emotional. You see me make a million mistakes, but your love is still there for heaven's sake. Thank you!!!

When the first man Adam realized he was alone, he went to his Creator and asked for a partner. God fulfilling all His children's requests created Lilith from dust to join Adam and to be by his side.

Lilith was a pure creation of cosmic energy who was full of strength. Lilith represents the dark goddess who travelled in the depths of the unknown, allowing us to go within our emotional self and trust our intuition. Lilith is the goddess who brings sexual healing power to those who feel weak in that domain. Lilith was the goddess of sacred sensuality who first came into creation at the temple of Inanna. Married to Adam, Lilith demanded equality, but Adam didn't believe in it. Adam was fixed in his own set of beliefs and demanded she be his helpmate. Lilith responded, " Why should I lie beneath you, when I am your equal? Both of us are created from dust to love one another."

Lilith refused to lie beneath Adam and Adam refused to be beneath Lilith. He believed she only fits him perfectly underneath and believed he was the superior one. So she should oblige.

Originally, Adam and Lilith were created from an image from God to manifest a happy life in the Garden. Lilith in disbelief couldn't believe that the man she was in love with only wanted sexual encounters if he was on top. This realization mortified her. His bruised ego pushed her off the mantel she believed she was on.

Lilith became awakened to the refusal of her husband who wouldn't meet her half way.

In that moment, she came to realize that he was on a search to feel superior and she couldn't justify it. Adam projected this anger on Lilith as he searched for his own lost innocence. She knew that until he found it, he found it he would treat her this way. With the two unable to agree upon anything, Lilith decided to grow wings and she flew away from the Garden to explore something more fulfilling. Feeling wild and free, Lilith flew away to the Sea of Reeds- a place where the Hebrews will once day be free from slavery. Ready for uninhabited places she goes. Adam was saddened by his wife's absence.

As Lilith pondered what to do, she looked him directly in his eyes, and he was unable to hide. Adam wasn't welcoming, so she cried. She took a deep breath, her strength was lost as he did not look at me while he spoke. He turned away and disregarded her every attempt. Fear built inside her but she didn't care, she picked herself up and walked away. She Knew that once she departed She would be judged for violating a sacred union created by God. She just couldn't stay.

Lilith, lay on the floor, eyes turned to the heavens. Her heart was open with total tenderness. She became disconnected, lost for words- mumbling to myself," I don't know what it feels like to live without pain. I was always being asked to tame my force but why couldn't I be accepted for whom I am? As I lay there, he didn't cuddle me. Instead he belittled me."

The feeling touched me. Then and only then did he see my despair- the true pain I felt as he cast me away to live a lonely life.

Adam spoke to his creator, stating that he as a man desired Lilith at his side and no longer wanted Eve. He felt that Eve was too naive.

Adam felt intrigued by a woman who stayed strong in her own strength and wanted her by his side. Adam asked God to bring Lilith back. However Lilith desires to release herself to a man who saw her for everything she is. She wanted to rise in his glory and not feel belittled by him.

Despite his desire for power, she still saw him for what he could be. Powerful, strong, equal, and open. Adam asked Lilith to have mercy on him for not understanding the ways of the world. Lilith, whose heart was broken, replies, "Dont expect this of me." Lilith continued, "Years later they made accusations about me for not allowing a man to mistreat me. Many believed I should have laid beneath him and accepted his advances because I was his wife. "Lilith only said," No! She hoped that it would mirror back what Adam denied, with hopes it would awaken him. Lilith wanted to reclaim her own wholeness and truth through divine light.

As she entered into marriage she didn't see them as separate. She wanted to be his guide through all his darkness and misconceptions he believed to be true about sacred marriage. Lilith Knew in my heart She'd never respect a man who cast her away. She was lost for words. Every corner she turned, all she felt was pain.

She was suffocated from the whims of masculinity. She was willing to accept him, that's why I married him. She wanted to lie there bare and take in all of him but could only give herself to a man who would not misuse me.

This went against the custom of the era.

She knew she would have had some pleasure, but she couldn't experience the ultimate pleasure if I had to submit completely while performing the act. Lilith says," I chose myself. I know darkness and light." Lilith was labeled as beautiful but then seen as a symbol who leads men astray. She only led him to equality Lilith says,"

She cried so deeply as the grief overwhelmed her. I walked, much further than I expected I could walk. The next day, she lay in the desert my heart into a million pieces. However, her pain turned into rage as she looked at her body burnt by the rays of sun. At that moment, her mind was spiralling out of control. However she knew she must find my home wherever that was. Lilith gently reminded of the words Adam said. "It is my house. You just live in it." Lilith replies," bit but it is our house Adam, like God & Goddess.

As she lay on the desert sand, wisdom found her. Out of nowhere, she heard the words. A woman never finds herself through being submissive or silenced. You have been created to be more than just a helpmate. She risked losing her relationship with Adam for equality.

Adam then revealed to God his wife was gone. God then sent three Angels to capture her and bring her back to the Garden Of Eden. Lilith wandered the Earth while Adam was stuck in his thoughts, wondering what he had done wrong.

Winging across the night sky, the Angels arrived. As they approached Lilith in the cave she was bearing twin children. Lilith, refusing to go with them was stunned, with the statement," Well kill your children should you disagree." Lilith felt so much mental abuse but she still didn't budge. Then the Angels said," we shall drown you.

Lilith, still holding her ground, refused and walked away. Lilith, simmering over her feelings decided to go back to the Garden. Imagine her surprise when she noticed Eve was there.

Lilith reminds us to embrace our essence. As you turn your face to the sun you reveal what is coming up for you today. Lilith Is the goddess we connect with when we feel abuse from our partner. She is the goddess who is a direct mirror of a woman's strength. Lilith is a direct reflection of a woman who was promiscuous not by choice, but couldn't bring herself to sleep with Adam under his terms. She shone the light on a divine feminine principle allowing us to see the darkness that rises from the shadows of ignorance as we try to honour duality.

She felt celibacy wasn't an option for her, but knew that sleeping with Adam wouldn't satisfy her because of the way he made her feel.

Lilith brings balance and eliminates shame revolving around a woman's sacred sexuality. Lilith calls you into the darkness of uncharted territories, to honour your truth. Many women were terrified to enter the darkness so for centuries they ran from it with the intention not to face it.

Lilith insists that since you are connecting with her right here, that you act accordingly and trust in your feelings. Never allow yourself to be trapped by notions of what you think you should do as your intuition will always guide you.

Before entering her cave you must know a woman's temple is to be entered with Respect & Reverence. As she walked on a trail fighting for equality, she discovered that many men will want to enter, but not all will be granted access.

The symbolism of witnessing a woman so strong in her wisdom is a metaphor for all women today.

As we look deeper into Lilith's story, it is safe to say that she felt, when it comes to intimacy between another and ourselves a woman's temple must be respected and adored. She must be made to feel like one of his most precious gifts, not a body that just lies beneath him out of his own need for power.

As women, we don't always hold the space to trust our inner voices. Somehow, we move away from our inner truth, but in those moments things never feel good. Sometimes, we bump into resistance and adapt this internal script that says, "I don't trust this feeling I feel within." We then wonder why we don't trust ourselves.

We've spent most of your life in the roles as teacher, mother, leader and nurturer who guides others. However it is hard for us to trust the guidance we would give others.

It is important to be centred and balanced within ourselves and our truth. To claim our voice with compassion and stand in our heart with our deserving feminine light. The time has arrived sweetheart to activate your blueprint and bring forth the healing heart of the goddess. Isn't it a special gift to be asked by the goddesses to enchant divine will, to harmonize our hearts and embrace the love and compassion of our souls.

Yes my loves, we are the chosen ones because the divine mother lives within us. Lilith has made her bed alongside Adam.Lilith is anchored in us. Every morning we wake up we leave room in our pathway for her that leads to the gates that loves unconditionally. It is time to unveil the goddess in you.

She is ready for your love my dear..

She is calling you.

She is waiting for your aliveness.

Curious to witness your contribution, she wants to feel your petals unfold..

You know that the sacred dance you do which contributes to the earth and loving humanity too.

She, the goddess has called you into her sacred heart. She holds space for you my loves and even when you feel like you are alone in an empty space, she is there with open arms. As I call out to the goddesses, I ask that their truth live out through me and carry on to my children and their children.

The goddesses' hearts are calling us to awaken- to slowly step fourth and claim the love in you that went hiding. That part of you which fell apart; or perhaps forgot her truth. The goddesses and our ancestors left behind an oath- an oath that asks us to carry love in our lineage and to hold this love in our DNA for all of humanity to feel.

If we listen, she lives in our hearts. She is with us every step of the way and in every breath we take. Every fibre that sheds from our soul is dusted upon her and memory that cannot be erased. In this voice of the goddess, we honour the masculine too, My loves, we do not exclude you, for many of you held the medicine that leads the way. You held the sacred Rose in your heart for her. You stood beside her so she could flourish. You went nowhere as she found her way. You carried her to the altar of self- love when you felt her fade away.

Mantra:

A woman's intuition is ancient wisdom passed down through the centuries.
The ancient ones who turned into their being through listening. Fully realizing and seeing that what they felt was worthy of listening.
She was always listening...
with modest confidence she believed in herself above everything else.
The red rose, (yoni) teaches us the sacredness of a woman's body.

Lilith

I will not bow down or kneel at his feet..
I believed in equality. I insisted that Adam & I, stand side by side. To free my spirit,
I fled the scene and landed in the arms of angels who carried me. I grew wings that carried me away, knowing it's the only way to honour myself. As I headed to the darkness, I walked for miles, crying the whole way. However, In my heart I believed that I am more than just a submissive servant. I knew so much pain. Pain, I would not have felt had my husband met me halfway. Yes, I sought revenge after years of torment.

Chanting to myself, I said.

"I am who I am and I do not need anyone's approval.
My dear speak your truth.
No one owns you.
You only share your heart willingly
with a man who treats you like a queen.
Adam and I made from the same dust.
Don't allow anyone to dominate you.
As the dark shadows unfold in our lives,
I bring strength, power and courage to you.

Chapter 18

● **Goddess Venus**

"Bathe In the rays of illumination" - Vange Cain

To you I bring a message of complete oneness. We are headed on a portrait that cleanses your mind, body and soul. Today we explore the sexual energies you hold within as you allow all misconceptions to fade away from your subconscious. Romantic matters are in the spotlight as Venus, the planet of love shows up for us. As we walk with her warm embrace I ask that you accept this love..As many of you have walked backwards, I hold the light that leads your way forward. I offer you the ability to see earth as it really is. The structure of her body was built on love not destruction. You are being asked to embrace the sacred feminine and bring her light forward to the forefront, in order to honour the sacred masculine. The masculine offers precise logical teachings if one will listen. Teachings of balance and fair love. As we accept this truth we come into alignment as one spiritual being made up of feminine and masculine energies. My darlings, there is no dividing us, we are one. This is why I say," make love to the chosen one

Part of letting go of misconceptions, is letting go of any fears you perceive to be true about the feminine and masculine. As fearing to love either side of the feminine and masculine is to deny aspects of love. When you fail to accept either sides of duality it disendowers your ascension process that bonds us, because I have been lifted up into the heavens with the higher ups and if you shall join us, you must balance your mind, body and spirit.

I ask you to remember a time in your life when all you felt was love. Maybe you even broke apart, but it lead to falling back together. A moment in time when you knew no pain. To accept this offer you must first, make love a firm existence in your reality. Love must become your priority. As you journey into the sacredness of the heart chakra you begin to pour out love. As I pull you onto the clay of my world I shall raise you, nurture you, love you and never let you go. I shall show you motherly love that is of pure natural beauty. My land is a tapestry with a beautiful landscape that has an array of comfort that unfolds before your very eyes. There you shall bear witness to the unfolding of the rose.

I invite you my darlings, to walk through the groves as you gaze into the blue light. This offer has been made to open your throat chakra. As you connect with your breath, hold the sapphire close to your heart, know that in that moment you are connected to all the divine offerings. Imagine taking time to pause, allowing things to be still, while lying on the grass and you feel Peaceful. Serene and Content. As you listen to me, you allow your inner most sacred feelings to come forth as you express what needs to be said and you feel what needs to be felt. Blue is the color of the heavens and directs our attention to a pure mind - the mind that is uncluttered by thought. As you accept these subtle vibrations, this is when you unfold the petals of your tangled emotions. You find the seat at the divine dinner table.

Memoire Of Babalon

Welcome to the memoir of Goddess Babalon.

What I shall reveal to you is of the cosmic energies that I pour onto you- which requires your full attention because what I shall reveal may appear shocking to some. You, my daughters shall become scholars of my teachings and I insist you Inform everyone. I ask you dear ones, to fall upon your knees and pray for understanding as I fall from the clouds to be with you. I arrive, because humanity has tried to pull us apart.

I want you to come to understand my divine rays of dark beauty that have been sheltered from you for thousands of years.

As you enter the sanctum, you shall bathe in the enchantment of my love. I call you now, because the present age is under the influence of the forces of evil and we must create safety and protection for all involved.

Within the mystical system of my teachings, we reach a final stage where he or she must cross the Abyss and I shall meet you there, beckoning my love because some of my daughters are completely blind. It all depends on who shall manifest this teaching.

The time is at hand to guide my daughters to the truth that lives forward and leads to an open eye. This impasse is broken by closed eyes and there has been a lack of love and understanding. The information sealed within me is that of the mystical quest to become one with the earth. I am the great mother goddess Babalon. I ride astride holding the reins representing the mascuiine and feminine. Create magic from the image of my teaching and you shall be anointed with the power you need to move forward - the daughter who hold love in their hearts and stare fear in the face.

I shall bring forth the rituals contained in my cup because I seek no end and I shall instruct those who wish to understand my name.

She shall come to me as I call out my daughter's name; declare that she is dedicated, heart to heart and she shall wander under the moon and know the mysteries of the serpent and inform her sisters that have been hidden away.

I arrive, bringing with me the material tears and the rose of Aphrodite and myself. You are about to become a scholar as I prepare your work.

I am BABALAN and you shall receive greatness under my instruction. All power is in my hands, swinging open the doors to all hope and power. I shall stride through the gates of hell bringing you through the flames to much more loving and safe land- grabbing all men and commanding that my daughters receive love and respect. Powers that receive manhood in my cup and my daughters shall shake from climax to climax. You who do not accept the gift of my love, turning a blind eye and seeing beyond my hearts offering shall extend her hand in the hour of harvesting her reward.

Let her declare, Ask for nothing; but for my love.

It will be an ordeal for many who don't understand me. I am the traveller, who lives between worlds who gathers her children and carries them across the Abyss to remove them from the land of illusion. I have arrived, with my consort Dumzid. We have to appear to represent the full expression of man and woman. I give him praise, for he has shed his love on the mantle of my yoni and the rose began to open as he carried me away. As I travel, I come to you now as I chant in a soft voice. I congregate all the children of the land whose heart is pure and lead them into pastures of love. I gather up all my sons & daughters and lead them into my waters of love as my womb has no depths to it. He was curious, to know, if the depths of my heart would open to him should he pour his love into my womb where he beckoned to know me more.

I rose from the soil to join forces with the masculine to create heaven on earth for my heavenly father. I am the alchemist whose breath kisses the fermented souls and turns them pure.

I give these kisses to my daughters and they become intoxicated from laughter and love. As I spread love, I pour my water into the canals that will create love. My daughters, let them look upon my cup- the cup that holds the blood of the rose, for its structure came from God. Anointed are the worthy who want to understand my mysteries. Please know my daughters, that we all came from the feminine womb where all men have space to rest. As you allow yourself to be swept away by the Abyss, know that you are protected by me and you are at home now wherever you are.

Day 1

● **Take Us to the Goddesses' Palace Where We Belong**

Today we are going to start our day with a prayer to our goddesses. Today we are going to tell ourselves, "I am so grateful for the wonderful and beautiful opportunities that consume me." Today we are going to squeeze every ounce of the goddesses' offerings into us so we feel abundance. "Thank you, goddesses, for this miracle work you've performed as you allow us to grow and heal gradually. The love you send us is deeper than any lake, ocean, or sea that we could ever be consumed in. Again, thank you, goddesses, for standing next to us."

● **Our Prayers**

"I am Enough."

Today we are going to start our day with a prayer to our goddesses. Today we are going to tell ourselves, "I am so grateful for the wonderful and beautiful opportunities that consume me." Today we are going to squeeze every ounce of the goddesses' offerings so we feel abundance. "Thank you, goddesses, for this miracle work you've performed as you allow us to grow and heal gradually. The love you send us is deeper than any lake, ocean, or sea that we could ever be consumed in. Again, thank you, goddesses, for standing next to us."

Day 2

● **Goddesses' Gift**

Today the goddesses want to sprinkle you with rose oil, so you will feel elevated, balanced, beautiful, and loved. And as you imagine this offering, I hope you bestow the love sent to you through your divine mother. Regardless if you are alone, or simply feeling alone, or if you are covered by the presence of loved ones, either way the goddesses say, "You deserve to feel loved."

Day 3

● **Our Garden**

I am a unified and beautiful
expression of the goddesses love.

Chloris, goddess of flowers, created the rose from a lifeless body of nymph. She understood she couldn't create such a masterpiece alone so she called on others to help, so she could dwell in their knowledge to bring the centerpiece to fruition. So today, the goddesses want you to create a new garden, so they will contribute a helping hand and even if you don't feel their presence they are there, helping you nature whatever your heart desires.

Day 4

● **Our False Start**

> "I am love, I am strength.
> I have courage.
> I am powerful.."""

Today or maybe even last week, you had a false start that led to your disappointment. You might even feel shame that surrounds this particular situation, and the goddesses understand because they too have endured some humiliating times. But they want you to know you are not at fault because these situations could have happened to any innocent heart. Today they ask that you may feel good about yourself and allow shame and humiliation to leave you, so you can unfold like a rose and then cast your love onto the world.

Day 5

● **Reach the Light**

Our soul has its own unique intention and its own yearning that is sometimes hard to fathom. But today the goddesses ask you to climb the mountain to reach your honor that comes from a safe place within our hearts. To reach Mount Olympus's mountain top, we must first start to open up and trust in our process and what is showing up. Your heart is screaming out for comfort, so let the light in to reach your mountain top.

Day 6

❋ My darlings

The Goddesses ask that you step into the mystery and take your place in their kingdom, becsuse since the beginning of time she has possed everything she needs within herself. it was the world that convinced her she did not. Since you are here I applause you for your courage to activate the wild sacred feminine inside of you. I ask that you use this book as a guide to harness the rhythms of the goddess. They will guide us to answer the question that guide us to tap into our purpose. To be in sync with our hearts and awaken our womb so we nourish ourselves and cultivate a beautiful life.

Day 7

❀ Skullcap

As beautiful as she is, this flower is potent, powerful, and fiercely designed to assist the goddess in you. The goddesses want you to benefit from this beautiful natural healing from Mother Earth so your heart can be healed. They want you to relish in calming your heart, mind, body, and soul so you no longer suffer from anxieties. When the wind blows, the goddesses show up to say, "Look inward for inner peace because you sway and open so beautifully."

Day 8

● **Sunflower**

Today the goddesses ask that you allow the sun to arrive in your path after you've embraced the dark shadows of the moon. Goddess Luna asks that you trust in her enough to light up your path. Today she sends you a sunflower so you can extract every ounce of vitality that you deserve. This sunflower, being infused in your life, will bring you spiritual growth and the juice you need to fuel your fire.

Day 9

● **Connect with your Mother**

The goddesses ask that you rekindle any harsh feelings you have toward your mother because as women, we're all put here to represent the divine mother within us. The divine mother is forgiving and loves from an open heart. The goddesses say, to deny your mother is to deny the existence of Mother Earth.

Day 10

❀ God's Counterpart

The goddesses want you to understand that you are not a mistake, and that you were purposely chosen from God's rib. The goddesses are calling you back to your roots where you first began. You are the representation of your partner's feminine aspects. We all have feminine and masculine polarities within us. Therefore, he may try to hide this aspect of himself. This is when you my darling, should love him from an open heart,, because you are the inspiration that leads the way.

Day 11

● **Take a Break**

As we activate the bridge of your heart. I pull you closer into complete alignment with love. As you offer your heart, the vastness of mysteries presents itself to you. My dear, the one who is ready to dissolve to the whims of love. She is ready to claim that today is her day to open her heart. Today (and everyday), I want you to remember that you were created to be the greatest version of the goddess. I love you my daughters, Hestia.

Day 12

● Pamper Your Soul

Spend the day with the goddess within. Nourish your soul by giving her what she needs. Cuddle up by a fire and explore your desires. Melt from the heat of the fire by allowing your breath to take you to places you never thought you could reach. The goddesses say it's time to elevate the goddess within by exploring deep within to find the answers they are ready to reveal to you.

Day 13

● **Splash of Water**

Today the goddesses ask that you forgive yourself for all the things that you feel are humiliating or degrading to you, because you are going to start over with them. Today they are splashing you with healing water so you can be purified and unashamed.

Day 14

● **Slow Down**

When the dust begins to clear, the confusion will fade. The goddesses ask that you take a moment to reevaluate your purpose and why it means so much to you. Doing this will keep your reminder in your mind as to why you even started your process in the first place.

Day 15

● **I Am Beautiful**

Today the goddesses ask that you make affirmations to yourself because you are what you believe.

Let's say

- I am beautiful.
- I have beautiful qualities, so there is no shame in being me.
- I have within my feminine essence—a strength and wisdom that can get me through all things.

- Today I am going to awaken the divine feminine essence that resides deep within me.
- Today I awoke to my soul's essence, so I enjoy the reunion of me.
- Yes, I unfold my petals so beautifully.

Day 16

❀ Emotional Power

There is a hidden secret inside of you, something you've never told anyone else.

It is a secret that makes you vulnerable that you try to hide, but you also can't fully rise into your light and be seen until you release that burden. Goddess Diana says you are a wild goddess—full of ideas and strengths. And her reflection from the moon protects you from needing to hide behind the shadows of your reflection. Step into the light and meet goddess Gaia there with so much love

Day 17

⚜ **Align Your Energies**

You are the primal spirit of life. It is a time of rebirth and new possibilities. Your chakras are the centerpiece to your goddess's life force. They draw in universal energies that bind to the goddess within you. Goddess Rhea says in order to align your channels, you must keep them flowing with ease.

Day 18

● **Thank Yourself**

We all go through life feeling like we could have accomplished more or changed a certain situation because we would have had better results. The goddesses say you've done a great job in your learning process, and it leads to your enlightenment. Today the goddesses ask you to thank yourself for the process you've made because they couldn't do a better job themselves. Thank yourself for your process because you are good and full of strength when it rains.

Day 19

❀ Hand in Hand

Sometimes you're going through hard times, and you're afraid to stretch your arms and admit you need some help. Goddess Gaia says as she nurtures the earth, we all need help to nurture our lives. She says be courageous and go for whatever is in the pit of your womb because that is where the truth lies.

Day 20

● **Meet the Goddesses**

The goddesses want to know how many blessings you are ready to receive. If they show up, will you surrender and trust the process of where they lead you today? Or will you resist and stay in your comfy, cozy place? In order to benefit from their love, you must believe in their process to see you through. I know it's hard to trust, but if you meet them at the altar, beautiful things await.

Day 21

● **Merge Energy**

Upon waking up today, let us look upon the goddesses so we can merge our energies with theirs as we divorce ourselves from the swinging gates that divide us from our true, authentic goddess selves. Today guide us to rise out of self-pity and the shame that hold our hearts back from flourishing into the most beautiful expression of ourselves.

Day 22

❋ Unclutter

Today the goddesses say it's a day for a new beginning. They are alongside you as you unclutter your life. They say you've been holding on to a lot of memories from the past, and it's time to let go. If you have photos of that special someone that you can't let go of, today is the day to put it in your goddess box and set it free from your heart.

Day 23

❀ Open Your Heart

Remember my dears, that a closed heart is shut, it is not able to let anything in or allow anything out. A closed heart is afraid to be open fully, due to it protecting itself. Maybe because it makes you feel vulnerable or exposed. The most beautiful parts of your being are the parts that no one knows. When we close the lid to the most sacred parts of ourselves how can light or love find its way in? Open up my dears and remember that life is energy. When we give love, it allows love to come back to us and when our heart is closed love detours the other way. We all have things about ourselves we wish we could change, but when you start to accept that our lives are created with divine love then and only then do we see that we don't need to protect ourselves so much. Allow yourself to feel empowered by this universal truth. My dears, there are no mistakes, just lessons that need to be lived through..

Day 24

● **Allow the Flow**

Today is the day to sit back and relax and allow the goddesses' energy to flow through you. They ask you to respond to the beautiful-changing circumstances that they want to lead you to. They want you to at least allow them to take you high as the sky, like a kite travels its way with the breeze. While you are sitting there, goddess Rhea pours milk upon your body to purify your soul.

Day 25

❀ Honour Yourself

For those of you who don't know this tiny bit of information I'm going to reveal, you will be delighted to open your eyes to the goddesses in their purest forms. There was a time that women were admired for being the birth-givers of the earth and for their sensuality, strength, and the ability to soothe the earth. Women received so much respect because they were the heartbeat that kept everything flowing with gentle ease. God was depending on them as the source of survival to direct the world. But somehow, we've drifted apart, feeling like we must give more of ourselves to be seen as the beautiful beings that we are. We forgot that stepping forth to shine our feminine light is not enough. We grew apart from our primal rhythms, and today we must unite, stand strong, and bring it all the way back to the ancient days, when we did less and when life was full of ease and beauty. Today is the day to honor yourself and love your every breath, for you are a goddess.

Day 26

❁ Arms of Shelter

The goddesses say that today is the day to have the courage to walk fearlessly into the arms of the goddesses who are patiently waiting to shelter you. A shelter that is warm and comfy that allows you to sink into the mysteries of yourself. They allow you to explore the possibilities of the awakened goddess within.

Day 27

⬤ **Meet Me by the Sea**

Goddess Yemeya has swum her way to the shore. Because she wants you to meet her by the sea so you can gather in love to connect heart-to-heart. Once you arrive, you will feel an array of love and warmth. She wants to understand your desires and concerns so she can help you overcome your obstacles. Once you arrive, a sea shell will be waiting for you to ignite your inspiration, evoke your courage, and spark your fire.

Day 28

❋ **Goddess Ritual**

The goddesses want you to make it a ritual that you join them in celebration to unite and rejoice with the goddess tribe to honor the love they have for you. It is time to walk the trails that bond our feminine hearts. Let's glide through the trails that take us up and away with them to a place of peace. This is our sacred, silent walk that will be the excitement that allows us to dream with them and explore new territories.

Day 29

● **Entrust in Him**

The goddesses say, "It is okay to entrust your feelings to your king.. It is the display of trust in him that you reunite and land in his arms. It is in this act of trusting in him that you experience the higher frequencies of love." Aphrodite, goddess of love, says, "It is okay for the goddess to collectively find peace at last." Aphrodite says you don't need to be trapped inside your mind, open up, awaken, and to feel his love at last.

Imagine you opening your hearts space to flow like a beautiful river, giving him stillness, shiver, gentle movement, erotic beauty, and flowing love. Feel yourself floating all the way to be in his arms. Do you feel the fur, the heat, and the strength? The more you float your way to him, the closer you become. This is the beautiful essence of the feminine entity. The more you open up, shed light, share love, cry a river, explain how you feel, love him, and trust in him, the more you will experience a spiral of spiritual journey from you to him. You will notice there is so much that he wants to reveal to you through these beautiful energies. Keep visualizing these beautiful energies and feel his love flowing like a river as he drifts his way to be with you. Feel his unconditional love and imagine the balance of spiritual love.

Day 30

● **Follow the Stars**

The goddesses say that today you must follow the stars to the abyss that holds so much love for you. Find your dreams my dears, no matter where you land just keep following the light. Go as high as you can and as long as it brings you bliss.

Author's biography

Vange is from Halifax, Nova Scotia and when she was 28 she loaded up her car and grabbed her two young kids and threw some clothing in the back of the car and decided to drive off. She ended up in Niagara Falls with 600 dollars and not sure where she was going to live, but she knew that God would provide a way.

Vange is a mother of two children, a boy and a girl and she has done the unthinkable.

When her daughter was in high school, grade seven to be exact, she took on five teenagers whom she felt needed her support. The first girl arrived when her daughter came home one day from school and said," There's a girl at the school who looks to be homeless." The very next day Vange went to the school to talk to the young girl. She asked her, "Where were her parents?" The girl revealed to me that her dad had passed away in jail so she wasn't able to live with him. She ended up moving in with her grandmother, but two short months later she found herself devastated when her grandmother passed away. As if that weren't enough to go through, the girl found herself living in the school, hiding from janitors. At such a young age she couldn't afford an apartment and women shelters didn't feel very inviting. At that moment, she just wanted a place to lay her head. So she ended up moving in with a man, but he passed away in his sleep. Then she had nowhere to go, so she found herself in the school.

Hearing her story it was clear she had nobody, so Vange asked the young lady to move in with her and her family. She stayed with her family for 5 years. This is just one story of the five young women and boys who lived with her family.

Might I add, she never received money for the teenagers. She took care of them out of her own pocket. Vange was drowning in bills, but she still held it together for them, because she felt she should take care of them.

Vange felt called to pursue life coaching and that somehow intertwined with her becoming the writer she is today. She began to write about her experiences and study the Goddesses.

She began to write books to inspire those who had lost hope. Vange has published four inspirational books that empower many today.

How the book came to be.

When Vange was a young girl growing up, as she navigated through school she learned traditional subjects such as science, English, French and math.

However, she and her classmates never learned how to love. They never learned how to love themselves through the enslavement processes of pain that hurt so much. Regardless if that pain was a rejection, abandonment or a failed attempt to pass a subject, she was still sensitive and never quite learned how to cope with it.

School never taught her how to love herself and many women struggle to find love from within, because they couldn't fathom what it even was. When our relationships took a turn for the worse, there was no guide and the advice most people gave us was," Leave him." But what if you wanted to hold on.? Inside herself she knew there was another way, but she wasn't sure how to obtain it.

What if you wanted to make it work? Despite society saying, "Run," but her heart said," Keep holding on." She was torn and that was when the Goddesses showed up to guide her home to love.

In my heart I felt I wanted to be the girl I needed to be as a girl for other women.

I wanted to teach women how to care for their bodies and to be that guide that helps you identify what you're feeling. So I created the book ' Unfold Your Petals'... a woman's guide to unfolding the petals to self- love... a safe place where the goddesses greet her actually where she is without asking her to change anything. However, she is invited to see things differently.. That was the Goddesses' simple request.

Information

Vange is a Writer, Model, Life Coach and motivational speaker.

Vange's mission is to build a new world... surely, but slowly dissolving the web of crises that weren't quite understood. Crises that we often blame ourselves for as we lack the understanding that everything that happens is a learning curve.

Vange pertains to this mission through moments of rethinking and deepening into growing within self and healing misconceptions within herself.

She breathes, she is calm, she is trusting and allows the goddesses wisdom to flow through her like a subtle ocean wave that calms us through the night. Vange has proven to herself that we as a collective can get to a place of love. She began to write to the audience who needed the Goddeses' love.

Vange's previous book has been showcased on the New York Times Sunday review, in 2017 referred to as a prominent attribute considered to be an inspiring read. Evangeline's book "As She Walked" will also be featured in the book exhibition 2021 in New York City. Evangeline was also hand-picked by book scouts for a write-up from The Book Walker March 2020.

Personal favourite quote-

I am a woman who believes in right and wrong.
I am a woman who talks to the earth while writing stories and singing songs.
I am a woman who believes everything can manifest love.
I am a woman who honours the earth as I walk barefoot.
I refuse to carry the sins of others in my heart.
I need nature as my oxygen to heal the world.
I am a woman whose love for creativity and wildness sparks my imagination to wander and I am a woman who sees nature as my medicine to heal the earth.

Journal

Journal

Journal

Journal

Journal

Journal

Journal

Journal

Journal

Journal

Journal

Lightning Source UK Ltd.
Milton Keynes UK
UKHW041333131021
392145UK00001B/249